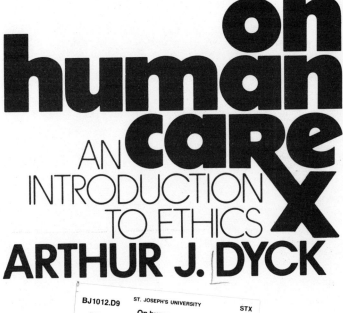

on human care

AN INTRODUCTION TO ETHICS

ARTHUR J. DYCK

ABINGDON
Nashville

ON HUMAN CARE: AN INTRODUCTION TO ETHICS

Copyright © 1977 by Abingdon

Library of Congress Cataloging in Publication Data

DYCK, ARTHUR J 1932-
  On human care.
  Includes bibliographical references and index.
  1. Ethics. I. Title.
BJ1012.D9   170   76-52490

ISBN 0-687-28845-2

Scripture quotations are from the Revised Standard Version Common Bible, copyrighted © 1973.

A portion of chapter 2 appeared in *The Monist* (January, 1977).

MANUFACTURED BY THE PARTHENON PRESS AT
NASHVILLE, TENNESSEE, UNITED STATES OF AMERICA

To

Sylvia, Sandy, and Cindy

contents

preface

Recently an eminent physician was quoted as saying that "ethics is not a science, it is an expression of the feelings of the majority." However accurately this quotation conveys the outlook of that particular physician, it is representative of some, but certainly not all, of the many physicians and health professionals with whom I have discussed moral issues of mutual concern. Furthermore, such a view is by no means confined to health professionals. What is not commonly recognized among those who think in this way is that they are taking for granted the truth of a particular ethical theory, not the most plausible one, as we shall argue, regarding the nature of ethics. And if ethics is perceived in this way to be in the domain of nonscientific considerations and to be expressive of emotional preferences rather than judgments of what is true and false, there will be little reason to think of ethics as a source of knowledge or enlightenment. What is to be gained from an introduction to ethics when, from this point of view, it is nothing more than an elaborate, rationalized expression of the author's own preferences, coupled with the desire to persuade others to share some of these same preferences? Why not instead read sociology and psychology to learn how most people feel?

This book invites professionals and others to examine ethics and to judge for themselves whether there is not something more to it than a sophisticated tract on behalf of certain emotional and intellectual biases. Indeed, I write with the hope that this book will clarify for its readers in what sense and to what extent ethics is a discipline from which knowledge, however modest, may be gleaned. I would not claim that the theories of ethics can be accepted and rejected with the same certitude some of the other sciences enjoy. Yet ethics is not devoid of precision and evolution in the refinement of its concepts and practical applications.

But there is more at stake in what that physician allegedly said and in what this book is trying to do. If one truly believes and acts upon the belief that ethics is the expression of the feelings of the majority, the implications of that are extremely serious, not only at the theoretical level, but also at the practical level. Held without qualification, such a view implies, for example, that racial discrimination, or even slavery, would be morally justified when it is an expression of the feelings of the majority, that theoretically, and hence also practically, there is no moral or ethical basis for questioning the will and preferences of the majority. Indeed, such a view provides no moral justification for any constitution that articulates the rights of each individual citizen and the obligation of government to protect such rights against the potential tyranny of individuals or groups. In any event, ethics and this book are concerned with examining the practical implications of particular beliefs regarding what is right and wrong, good and evil. A major purpose of this book is to make people aware of their own most deeply held moral beliefs and the implications of these beliefs for their behavior and the behavior of others.

Ancient religious and philosophical traditions throughout the world have carried on increasingly systematic inquiry into our judgments regarding what is right and wrong and the extent to which we can offer justifications for such judgments. Along the way, methods of inquiry and concepts have developed that may be usefully applied in trying to decide questions of morality and questions of public policy. This book also seeks to acquaint the reader with some of these most basic methods and concepts so that they may be reflected upon and if found worthy, used and applied as the occasion arises.

This book, then, has not less than three purposes: to introduce ethics as a discipline, to acquaint readers with some examples of the extent to which ethics offers guidance for practical understanding and moral decision-making, and to introduce methods and concepts for this purpose. This book intends to stimulate readers to make moral decisions that are congruent with their most deeply held moral values, those they share in great part with other human beings. The author recognizes continuing debate and differences of judgment regarding what these are and how widely they are held. As in any field, the benefits of what ethics has learned are not contingent on complete agreement or lack of controversy. Indeed, every gain in knowledge depends heavily on arguments and counterarguments, especially in ethics.

For accomplishing these purposes, I have used concepts, methods, and substantive thought drawn from both moral philosophy and religious ethics. In this respect, at least, I think this introduction is rather unique, for it prepares the reader for further study in both these fields without presupposing any prior training in either. I have not limited myself simply to summarizing the views of others, though I try to cover as accurately and fairly as I can a range of thinking on the subjects discussed. Of course, I make no claim to have done this perfectly or to every reader's satisfaction. To encourage debate and thought, I have usually argued the merits of certain points of view so as to engage the reader directly in the enterprise of ethics and also be explicit about the direction of my own thinking.

The substance of this book has in large part been gleaned and refined from over ten years of introducing ethics to under-graduates and to graduate students in the Graduate School of Arts and Sciences, the Divinity School, and the School of Public Health at Harvard. I owe a great deal to all the students with whom I have engaged in so many animated discussions and debates. Many changes that I consider salutary have stemmed from these many contacts with bright, inquiring, and often well-informed young minds. Without the constant encouragement to publish a volume of this sort from so many of my students, this book might never have been conceived or brought to fruition.

The most immediate goad to write this introduction to ethics came from the invitation to provide introductory lectures in ethics for health professionals at Georgetown University, and for military professionals at the War College in Carlisle, Pennsylvania. The effort to expose these professionals to ethics and to provide enough substance to entice them into and prepare them for further ethical reflection meant that I was forced to make the kind of selection out of the vast material of more than two thousand years of ethical reflection that a readable introduction to ethics requires. I doubt whether I could have been persuaded to undertake such a venture without the strong encouragement of Robert Cooke, Eunice Kennedy Shriver, and Sargent Shriver, all of them acting out of personal conviction and on behalf of the Kennedy Foundation, whose idea it was to provide an entrée to ethics for busy but highly motivated health professionals, some of them clinicians, some administrators, some researchers, and most of them teachers in their own respective fields. I would neither have been prepared nor persuaded had it not been the case that Dr.

Cooke himself attended an introduction to ethics I gave at Harvard. His persistent inquiries helped me adapt and refine what I was doing, and his insistence that he had gained something from this experience gave me the courage to undertake that course in Georgetown and ultimately this introduction. I owe him much.

I am equally grateful to Colonels Kermit Johnson and William Rawlinson for their insistence that military personnel at the rank of colonel need to know something about what both of them call "the basics" in ethics. I must say that I have been deeply impressed and inwardly moved by the experience of engaging in serious moral inquiry with military men and women who, more than most of us realize, are deeply concerned that truth and justice prevail within their profession. The frank support of the Commandant of the War College, General Smith, helped dispel my lingering hesitation as an utter novice to the ways of the military.

If this book has an unduly optimistic flavor for some of its readers, I can only confess to a certain exhilaration that I feel in writing a book in ethics that flows out of so much exposure in the past two years to professional men and women of great integrity and of sensitive conscience with whom it has been my privilege to take up the perennial questions of ethics. Behind all the stereotypes, accusations, and crisis-oriented exposés of mistakes and wrongdoing of military and health professionals, there is a relatively quiet but large cadre of honest, high-minded, and responsive professionals who will, I think, be heard from more and more. And like the students who have taught me so much, their language will increasingly be the discourse of morality and ethics, and it will be to a greater extent than ever before an educated and disciplined discourse.

In addition to the spiritual and moral support that the Shrivers have been to me, they have through the Kennedy Foundation also assisted me directly in a financial way. The Foundation has supported the most superb secretarial and editorial assistance anyone would hope to have in Ilse Fersing. She has been much more than a rapid and flawless typist and proofreader. She has provided the major source of specific suggestions for making the manuscript clear and readable for those who have never formally studied ethics. These few words hardly express my appreciation for her invaluable aid.

I am profoundly grateful to Richard and Mary Saltonstall. Their warm encouragement and generosity undergird all that I do and make it possible.

Among my teachers, my intellectual debts to Roderick Firth are particularly great and are extended now as colleagues beyond our first encounter in his excellent course in ethics which he continues to offer at Harvard. This is rather evident in chapter 7, but chapter 6 is also heavily dependent upon analyses that Roderick has made, most of these not as yet in published form. James Luther Adams and John Rawls are past and continuing mentors as well. Nor could I detail the countless ways in which the ethicists Paul Ramsey and James Gustafson and my more immediate colleagues Preston Williams, Ralph Potter, Stanley Reiser, and William Curran enrich what I do and think.

All persons owe their own parents a debt they can never adequately repay, namely, the gift of life itself. But I owe my own parents, who I am happy to say are still living, much more. In firm but loving ways, they have insisted that I be moral and that I know why. Everyone should have that kind of introduction to life and to ethics.

And, finally, how can words express my appreciation to my own immediate family, to whom this book is dedicated. The writing of it has been part of the rhythm of play and work established within our family, and it shares some of what we have learned together as a small, intimate community and as part of that larger community that all of us participate in as human beings. With enthusiasm and boundless energy, my twin daughters, Cindy and Sandy, make certain that what I do and what I say from a moral and ethical standpoint is practical, viable, and part of the very fabric of our daily lives together and with others. To share so intimately and completely my life with Sylvia, my companion in marriage, is to assure that ethics is never for me exclusively a scholarly vocation but an extension of life which in turn extends again into life. There is no way for me to know how deeply and extensively her tactful wisdom, example, and insights are part of anything in this book that is good. Of one thing I am sure, I owe her much.

chapter i
introduction

The noted English philosopher A. C. Ewing began his introduction to ethics by addressing his readers as follows:

> You, reader, whoever you are, are not a complete beginner in this subject. You already have some idea what "good" and "bad," "right" and "wrong" mean, and you know some acts to be right, others wrong, some things to be good and some bad. Now these are precisely the topics with which Ethics as a subject of systematic study deals.[1]

Now I also begin with the view that no one reading this book is a complete beginner in ethics. Many questions that arise constantly in the course of our daily lives are the selfsame questions to which ethics, too, seeks answers. Some of them, in medicine for example, are pressing in upon us with special urgency during the present era. As we shall see, these questions are systematically identified and pursued by ethics from within its major subdivisions—namely, normative ethics, metaethics, and moral policy.

NORMATIVE ETHICS

Normative questions are questions about what things are right or wrong, good or bad, virtuous or evil. Perhaps the reader is surprised that such questions are raised in ethics. How, you may ask, do these questions compare with the kinds of questions I ask as a scientist, perhaps, or generally, as a rational human being?

For the ethicist, trying to identify what kinds of things are right or wrong is, in fact, very much like the scientific enterprise of looking for the basic bits of existing matter out of which other matter can be made. And just as the physical world is made up of certain constitutive elements, so also is the world of moral discourse made up of certain constitutive elements.

Now in the search for constitutive elements in ethics, two types of theory have emerged: utilitarian and formalist. What divides these two theories is quite analogous to one of the divisions that occurs in the natural sciences. Utilitarian theory, for example, is quite like atomic theory and is not without considerable attraction because of it. If you look for the basic element or elements out of which all moral assertions or claims can be compounded, then anything that can properly be called right would have this element or these elements. The basic element for the utilitarian is utility. And what constitutes utility? As specified by John Stuart Mill, a leading utilitarian, utility is happiness, that is, the best balance of pleasure over pain. The right act is the act that will bring about the greatest happiness for the greatest number, or the best balance of pleasure over pain on the whole. What makes the utilitarian view so appealing is that it allows us to decide between alternatives simply by quantifying our judgments. How much pleasure and how much pain for how many people will be produced by a given action or policy? It is calculations of this sort—determining the quantity of pleasure and pain produced by realizing one set of values rather than another—that can then be used to decide among conflicting actions or policies.

But the quest for constitutive elements in our moral judgments can also be carried out quite differently. In the natural sciences, in addition to atomic theory where everything is reduced to one constitutive element, there is also the enterprise of describing elements that actually exist in nature as it is naïvely experienced and that provide data for various ecological types of theory. Such an enterprise has somewhat of a parallel in ethics in formalist theory. Formalism identifies as constitutive elements of our moral world certain bonds that actually exist among people, bonds that are imputed to be of moral significance in our daily, ordinary relations to one another. Formalists look at the context in which moral judgments arise, and it leads them to examine interpersonal relations, relations between individuals and within and between groups. People relate to one another by making promises or by expectations of finding out what is true. Your expectation, for instance, in reading this book is that I will not lie to you, that you can trust me to tell the truth to the best of my knowledge and ability and to be honest about what I do not know or understand. That is part of the bond between us at this moment. There are other bonds among people—those defined by the way in which we distribute goods and services, for example. In any event, the fact that our lot can be better or worse in relation to others, the fact that we have made promises, the fact that we expect the truth in

communicating with one another—all of these are morally
significant elements in our relations to one another. These are the
kinds of elements that characterize our moral world and that
specify the right- or wrong-making characteristics of actions.
Keeping promises is right-making; breaking them is wrong-
making. Telling the truth is right-making; lying is wrong-
making.[2] Identifying these morally significant kinds of bonds
among people is much like identifying the elements comprised in
a table of elements, the basic kinds of matter out of which all other
kinds of matter are compounded, derived, or manufactured. But
whereas the table of elements and atomic theory are both
distinctly useful in the natural sciences, the status of utilitarian
and formalist theories in ethics is not quite so clear and tidy. As
we shall see later, each of these theories seeks to encompass the
other.

The quarrel between utilitarianism and formalism is especially
urgent today within the practice of medicine. The professional
codes of modern medicine, for instance, clearly specify the
primacy of physicians' obligations to their individual patients. But
with the increasing application of utilitarian cost-benefit analyses
to social policy, there is a great deal of pressure upon medical
professionals to make judgments as to who will be treated and to
what extent, based on considerations of utility rather than, as a
formalist would insist, on the basis of the needs of those who seek
professional care and the skills of those who provide that care.
Some would argue that cost-benefit analyses have no place, by
and large, in the care of individual patients. Others would agree but
would at the same time assign a significant role to such analyses
for determining social policy for the whole society in the health
sphere. Still others appear ready to apply cost-benefit analyses to
the care of individual patients. This occurs, for example, when
physicians decide to try to persuade people not to give birth to or
not to try to save, through medical intervention, children who are
expected to be mentally retarded, on the grounds that the care of
the retarded is costly while the benefits of their existence are
minimal if, indeed, they are even seen as benefits to the children
or to others at all. The question concerning the moral basis of the
primary obligation of physicians, then, mirrors the competing
claims within normative ethics of utilitarian and formalist
theories.

METAETHICS

While in the section above we were discussing specific claims by ethicists that pleasure or truth or promise-keeping, and the like, are right-making characteristics of actions, you may have been asking yourself how one can justify identifying these characteristics rather than others as right-making. Within ethics, we call this a metaethical question.

Metaethics is an examination of the nature and use of moral language, of the very judgments and claims that are made in the name of right or wrong, good or bad, virtue or evil. People make judgments, for example, claiming that a specific action or policy is morally right or wrong, and they appeal for support of that action or policy by identifying what they consider to be its right-making characteristics. They may insist that what they have decided to do is right because it will prevent pain or fulfill a promise or increase justice, as the case may be. And as we noted above, this concern with identifying, specifying, and refining right- or wrong-making characteristics of actions or policies comprises the realm of normative ethics. Metaethics, then, seeks to know whether the moral judgments identified as such in normative ethics convey knowledge and, if so, what kind of knowledge. Do these judgments as to what is right or wrong and as to what characteristics are right- or wrong-making admit of truth or falsity? Is it appropriate to speak of such normative judgments as correct or incorrect, justified or unjustified, and if it is, how does one go about correcting or justifying such judgments?

Metaethical theories can be roughly divided into two types: noncognitivist and cognitivist. Noncognitivist theories restrict or virtually eliminate moral discourse as a source of knowledge. Emotivists, for instance, claim that moral judgments convey only a certain distinctive attitude of the person or persons making them. They reject the notion that moral judgments admit of truth and falsity. Other noncognitive theories, though in agreement that moral claims do not admit of truth and falsity in the strict sense, would argue that it is possible, however, to assess whether such claims are more or less reasonable. These theories generate certain criteria by means of which the rationality of moral judgments can be evaluated.

Cognitivists, on the other hand, argue that normative judgments do admit of truth and falsity. Intuitionists, for example, see certain moral claims as rationally self-evident. Naturalists are cognitivists who make the special claim that an analysis of moral discourse will yield empirically verifiable criteria by means of which the correctness or incorrectness of normative assertions can be judged.

Though we will be examining the credibility and implications of these various metaethical theories in a later chapter, it is important that the reader not misunderstand the issues being raised within metaethics. The question as to whether it makes sense to speak of moral judgments as true or false is not a question about certitude. Ethicists are well aware of the great difficulties of discovering truth in ethics, and they are not prone to making claims of absolute or high degrees of certitude for normative judgments.

That metaethical thinking is not at all remote from our daily lives should hardly be surprising. All of us make assumptions about the nature of ethical judgments; and even if we are not formally explicit, we still unwittingly represent one or the other of the existing metaethical options. Some professionals, for example, including medical professionals, take the view that professional judgments are not moral judgments. To make the correct judgment, on this view, requires that one accurately interpret the dictates of medical science, law, national security, or whatever the case may be. Such a view excludes from professional judgments not only ethics but our ordinary sensitivities regarding right and wrong, good and bad, virtue and evil, as well. There are clear assumptions being made here about what counts as knowledge, or at least relevant knowledge, in deciding questions about the health, well-being, and rights of the people who come under professional care. There are other professionals who would not deny that they do and should make moral judgments as professionals. Some of these professionals, however, take a distinctly noncognitivist attitude toward such judgments, considering them to be purely private, or emotional, or in any event, not subject to rational scrutiny. Others are much more inclined toward cognitivism and put a great value upon arriving at moral judgments through disciplined reflection of their own and/or through seeking counsel or debate. In short, then, some professionals are inclined to think of moral judgments as neither true nor false; others are inclined toward the opposite view.

MORAL POLICY

All of us, professionals or others, regardless of our opinions about ethics, encounter perplexities in trying to decide what is right or wrong. Technical developments in medicine are one source of such perplexities. Never before in human history has medicine had such efficient and powerful techniques for sustaining bodily functions. As a result, medical professionals are increasingly uncertain about the extent to which these techniques should be employed. For example, when are people to be put on respirators to keep the heart and lungs going when the brain is apparently irreparably damaged? How long should patients be kept on respirators when it appears that major functions of the brain will not be recovered? Understandably, we wonder how ethics can be of any help to us in these and other particular situations.

When faced with deciding between two or more alternative actions or policies, we are quite convinced of the need to learn as much as we can about the nonmoral particulars of the situation in which alternative courses of action present themselves. The quest for sheer information is not just a product of a scientifically and technologically minded age; it is first and foremost one of the responses we deem reasonable in seeking to decide what is right or wrong. Indeed, the successes of science, and of the professions that cultivate scientific expertise, may tempt many to act as though determining what is right or wrong is largely, if not exclusively, a process of discovering the most that one can about nonmoral facts. Anyone inclined toward this view expects little, perhaps nothing, in the way of guidance in trying to ascertain what is right or wrong from moral reflection or from the field of ethics as such. It is not surprising, therefore, that policy-makers in the modern era have increasingly sought technical advice and counsel from experts in the various natural and social sciences but not, as a rule, from those schooled in ethics. More positive attitudes toward expertise in ethics seem to be developing, but the point being emphasized is that most people, policy-makers included, need no convincing that certain technical and nonmoral knowledge is an important input into decisions as to what is right or wrong, good or bad. What, then, can the ethicist contribute in the formation of policy?

During the height of the debates regarding the morality of United States policy in Vietnam, Ralph Potter examined the concern he shared with fellow ethicists to be contributing something "relevant" at a time of profound agony over policy questions. He noted that "it is frequently supposed that to be relevant one must advance or advocate specific recommendations for public policy. What authority can the ethicist claim at this level of endeavor?"[3]

Based on a previous analysis of nuclear-arms policy debates and on his subsequent analysis of debates about Vietnam war policy, Potter drew the following conclusions about the nature of policy recommendations.

> Recommendations for what should be done here and now represent complex judgments. Every statement which proposes a policy by specifying a responsible agent, a goal, and an appropriate means for its realization is derived through a complex reasoning pattern which may conveniently be analyzed into four elements. In some cases, each element is made explicit. More frequently, one or more of the ingredients of policy thought are left implicit.[4]

Potter identified the following four elements: an empirical definition of the situation; affirmations of loyalty; some mode or modes of moral reasoning; and quasi-theological beliefs, particularly assumptions concerning the range of human freedom and the extent of human power to predict and control historical events and human destiny. Although there are certain systematic interrelations among all four of these factors that inevitably arise in the process of formulating policy, each of the four components is independently variable. This means among other things that one cannot predict either the content of any one of these elements or the policy that would result from it through knowledge of any combination of the other components. To understand a suggested policy, each of its four components would need to be examined.

Potter drew three implications from the kind of analysis that he discovered and applied to policy recommendations and debates:

> 1. There can be no "non-moral view" of [policy]. . . . Secular strategists may prefer to avoid the traditional vocabulary of moral discourse, but they cannot avoid making assumptions regarding ethical methods and norms. . . .

2. There can be no "purely moral view" of policy. No detailed recommendations flow simply and directly from the realm the ethicist commands as an ethicist. Authorities in the field of ethics share the plight of other experts. When they move beyond the limited area of their own special competence to formulate policy recommendations, they must, at their own risk, incorporate data drawn from the realm of other men's expertise. Their professional authority is adulterated and they properly become subject to the critical scrutiny of disciplined experts and undisciplined laymen. . . .

3. . . . The elements of policy thought are systematically interrelated. If, then, one brings about a significant change in one sector, the entire pattern will be modified. The ethical element is a particularly potent source of change, for it largely determines the logical structure of a chain of policy argument and the weight to be assigned to the considerations deemed pertinent. To change the way men think about what is right and wrong in [policy-making] is to exert a powerful, if somewhat indeterminant, influence upon the course of policy.[5]

An analysis of the type we find in Potter's work suggests two important ways in which ethics can contribute to individual decisions and policy recommendations. First, ethicists, as illustrated by Potter's work, can provide descriptive and critical analyses of the sources of agreement and disagreement as to what to do in specific situations. Second, if Potter's analysis is correct, the distinctive contribution of ethics will come from its efforts to refurbish and upgrade moral reasoning with respect both to what characteristics of situations will be regarded as right- or wrong-making (normative ethics) and what criteria will serve to render our moral judgments reasonable (metaethics), so that we act in concert with, rather than in defiance of, our own most deeply held values and so that these values, in turn, are subjected to self-conscious scrutiny. Chapter 2 is an example of the first kind of enterprise within ethics. In this particular instance, the categories developed by Potter are applied to current debates over the nature and need for population policies. The second kind of enterprise in ethics, concerned with how normative and metaethical thinking contribute to the formation of policy as well as to individual decision-making, will be evident not only in chapter 2 but throughout the remainder of our book.

ETHICS AS A DISCIPLINE

We have claimed that the major questions of ethics—questions about the inputs into our individual and policy decisions, questions about what kinds of things are right or wrong, good or bad, and questions about whether or to what extent we can justify or correct our moral judgments—are questions that come up for all of us. And whether we realize it or not, our actions betray certain answers to them. We have also claimed that the primary concern of ethics as a discipline is to ask these questions in as precise and as thorough a manner as possible and to test the kinds of answers that are and should be given to them. How does ethics do this? And how is it distinguished from other sciences or disciplines?

In a very general way, ethics can be defined as systematic reflection upon human actions, institutions, and character. But, you will say, there are a number of sciences concerned with the study of human actions, institutions, and character, with what people do and say, with how institutions work, with the kinds of needs, goals, and dispositions people have—psychology, sociology, economics, to name but a few. What distinguishes ethics from other sciences dealing with human behavior and institutions, however, is its interest not simply in what individuals and groups do and how they behave but in what they *ought* to do and how they *ought* to behave. Ethics asks about what is right or good or virtuous; it seeks also to identify and characterize moral arguments, and to investigate whether and the extent to which these arguments, or the decisions they are intended to justify, are rationally warranted.

Like other sciences, ethics is also interested in what we could call causal explanations or correlations, the whole question of what leads to what, the kinds of questions that are best characterized by the word *why*: Why is a certain event happening, or what has led to this particular set of phenomena or results? But when ethics asks the question why, it is primarily interested in justification. Individuals and groups make moral claims for their behavior. Ethics wants to know on what grounds these claims are made? What reasons are offered or can be offered for them? How reasonable or sound are these claims?

Ethics as a discipline, then, is a systematic analysis of what things are right or wrong, good or bad, virtuous or evil (normative ethics); of what is meant or conveyed by these moral terms to see whether or to what extent judgments involving them can or cannot be rationally justified (metaethics); and of specific moral decisions and policies, and what ethics can contribute to such decisions and policies (moral policy). Its basic methods of analysis are drawn from philosophy, theology, and, to some extent, the social sciences.

But ethics is also carried on within particular religious groups, professions, and philosophical systems; and groups of this sort often claim to have their own "ethic." I think it is important to say something about the difference between the study of ethics from a general perspective and the study of ethics as it occurs within these various groups. People are understandably concerned about whether ethics is a partisan effort, that is, whether ethics can only be taught from a particular point of view, one that cannot be easily identified or objectively criticized by others who do not share the viewpoint of a particular teacher or group representing ethics as a field. But to consider ethics as a form of special pleading or vested interest is, I think, unfair, or at least misleading, as the following discussion is intended to illustrate. I will examine first the relation between philosophical ethics and religious ethics and later take up the relation of medical ethics, as one kind of professional ethics, to ethics generally.

Interestingly enough, the positions taken regarding the relation between philosophical and religious ethics look like a table of logical possibilities. There are people who argue that ethics is encompassed by religious ethics. Others claim that ethics is encompassed by philosophical ethics. Still others assert that there are two kinds of ethics—one religious, the other philosophical. Last, there are those who view ethics as one, and who see religious and philosophical ethics as subheadings, or subspecies, of a single discipline of ethics.

To support their contention that ethics is encompassed by religious ethics, certain representatives of Christian ethics argue that it is only within Christian ethics that the good is known. Paul Lehmann, for example, states that Christians and Christian ethics begin with and presuppose knowledge of the good (God), while for philosophical ethics such knowledge is a problem.[6] The conclusion drawn from this is that the only correct ethics, and the only standard of what is correct in ethics, has to come from Christian ethics. After all, Christian ethics is grounded in revelation, the product and guide of the Christian community which yields special insight into the nature of what is good. Any study of ethics in which knowledge of God is assumed to be problematic or outside the scope of ethics is not capable of developing a complete understanding of what is good.

The second position, that ethics is encompassed by philosophical ethics, is one that is widespread in philosophy and clearly represented by William K. Frankena in his book *Ethics*. "Ethics is a branch of philosophy; it is *moral philosophy* or philosophical thinking about morality, moral problems, and moral judgments."[7] Just as some Christian ethicists would suspect, Frankena, in their view, makes a problem out of the good by distinguishing the quest to know the good from the quest to know God. He espouses the view that for those who employ the philosophical method for discovering what is good, the questions as to whether God exists and in what form are questions that he cannot and need not take up within his book on ethics. So Frankena self-consciously separates from ethics precisely what Lehmann, representing one view of Christian ethics, considers to be the starting point and essential working assumption of the ethical enterprise.

The third position, that ethics is twofold in nature, is represented by Aquinas, for example, who saw Christian ethics and philosophical ethics as distinct yet valid sources of knowledge as to what is virtuous or good. Certain virtues are known by the special community, that is, the Christian community. These are faith, hope, and love. These are understood by theology. Other virtues, namely, justice, prudence, temperance, and fortitude, are known by reason and are properly understood by philosophy. According to Aquinas, then, we have two sources of knowledge regarding right and wrong, virtue and vice.

This position is not limited to medieval times or to Roman Catholic traditions. The twentieth-century Protestant Reinhold Niebuhr is a distinguished representative of a view like that of Aquinas.[8] He separated love and justice as moral standards, love being a nearly impossible ideal known only by revelation, while justice is a more realistic, calculating ideal known by reason.

Last, there are those who argue that ethics is one. As a matter of fact, it was Reinhold Niebuhr's brother, H. Richard Niebuhr, who took this position, asserting that Christian ethics is a species of ethics.[9] Philosophical ethics is also a species of ethics generally. It stems from Greek traditions and continues self-consciously to draw upon those traditions.

The presupposition of this book is that ethics is one and that religious ethics and philosophical ethics are subspecies of ethics. The intent, however successful, is to introduce and exhibit the kind of disciplined reflection characteristic of ethics as a single, broadly conceived entity. We will certainly draw upon and use philosophical methods as well as certain kinds of systematic analyses that come to us from other sources, not only religious traditions, but also other disciplines where it seems appropriate or necessary to the subject of ethics.

The various positions as to what the relation is or should be between the ethics of special-interest groups and ethics generally occur also within discussions of medical ethics. You have people who argue that only physicians qua physicians know the good in medicine, that ethics cannot teach physicians anything about what is ethical in medicine since that has to be judged exclusively by physicians, that is, by those who have the training and experience. The medical profession is seen as a special community whose insights come from academic medicine—medical school, residence training, and the like—and from actual clinical experience with patients. And if we are talking about medicine as a science, the training and experience that come through research confer special insight that cannot be gleaned from or known to ethics as a field. A special community is the source of insight, of revelation as it were; and ethics outside this community has no access to this source. This position within medical ethics parallels the views expressed within the broader framework of ethics by the Christian ethicist Paul Lehmann.

A second position in medical ethics is that of Dr. Franz Ingelfinger, editor of *The New England Journal of Medicine*,[10] who has argued for a kind of dualistic theory like that of Aquinas and Reinhold Niebuhr. People trained in ethics can and should formulate general guidelines and try to specify some of the parameters of medicine and social policy. So there is a sphere, according to Ingelfinger, in which ethics does have something to say to and about medicine. But when it comes to specific issues or policies that concern us all as human beings, such as who shall live and who shall die, it is not ethicists who should make or even provide insight into these decisions. Rather, physicians should do so. Who else can comfort, who else can explain, who else knows the condition of the patient? Parents, ministers, relatives—none of these people is mentioned as having any kind of expertise or warrant for making decisions about people who are dying. Yet, it is quite understandable that professionals who accumulate special knowledge, as well as experiences associated with care for the dying and care for grieving relatives and friends, should feel that special insight or revelation in such matters belongs to the medical community. Ethics, accordingly, may have a place in formulating general guidelines, but the decisions about specific cases are illuminated and/or understood not by ethics generally but by medical professionals. This is the equivalent of a two-kingdom theory, where ethicists are confined to one area and physicians to another, of valid but different expertise and sources of knowledge.

A third position is that medical ethics, like religious and philosophical ethics, is a subspecies of ethics generally. Edmund Pellegrino, for instance, is a physician who wants health professionals to receive training in ethics as a discipline on the grounds that its knowledge and the insights gained are relevant and will enrich both their understanding and practice of medicine.[11] It is this view that corresponds with the working assumption of this book. Medical ethics, like religious ethics and philosophical ethics, constitutes a distinctive body of thought and practice. But at the same time, it raises questions and employs methods systematically pursued and analyzed by ethics as a discipline.

At this point, I think it is only fair to mention that plausible objections can be raised with respect to the position I am adopting. But I do not really believe it is important in an introduction to ethics to debate the view that religious ethics, philosophical ethics, medical ethics, and the ethics of other interest groups and professions exhibit and benefit from the systematic ethical reflection that has been carried on within philosophy and theology for a number of centuries. The position I am taking does not rule out the possibility that in a strict sense, it is an erroneous one from the point of view of some particular religious group, professional group, or other interest group. What I do assume, however, is that insight can come from any one or combination of these sources and that an introduction to ethics should adopt some pragmatic framework in which various points of view and methods of doing ethics are not excluded by the working assumptions of the author. Such a position would seem a good heuristic device. To provide detailed arguments in support of such a pragmatic and open approach to ethics, however, would take us too far afield since such arguments are part of a long history of debate far beyond the scope of the present volume. Suffice it to say that typically the introductions to ethics that I have seen presume that ethics is a part of philosophy, which it is, or a part of theology, which it is, or is separately contributed to by both. Little or no allowance is usually made for positions other than the one adopted, even though it would be apparent on reflection that adopting any one of these three assumptions about the nature and scope of ethics tends to exclude what others have thought to be part or even the whole of ethics as a discipline. It is this tendency that the present book seeks to avoid, though without any pretense to do so perfectly.

WHY STUDY ETHICS?

So far I have indicated some reasons people might be inclined to pursue the study of ethics. In the first instance, illustrations from the area of medical practice indicate that the kinds of questions characteristic of ethics are surreptitiously or even forthrightly raised within our daily lives and within the course of our vocational and professional obligations. Second, readers have been assured that ethics is a systematic discipline in its own right and that ethicists have given more time and thought to moral questions raised within our common life than those who have other specialties have time to give to them. But none of us has time to study everything, and the fact that we have limited time and important specialties to pursue makes us wonder whether we should pursue yet another discipline. Such doubts are understandable and even morally responsible insofar as everyone has exacting obligations. Yet, although I agree with Ewing that all of us *know* "some acts to be right, others wrong, some things to be good and some bad," at the same time this implies that there are some acts that we do not know to be right or wrong and some things we do not know to be good or bad. In fact, as I intimated earlier, some of us may doubt that we can "know" anything in any significant sense of "knowing" what is right or wrong, good or bad. Why, then, study ethics?

It is not enough to appeal to your intellectual curiosity, although that may be enough to attract some readers to this book and to lead them to complete it. It is not enough because people are curious about many things, not all of which they can or should pursue. The question facing all of us is whether it is rational to cultivate an increased awareness of our own acting and thinking. Since all of us unavoidably make judgments about what is right or wrong, good or bad, and these judgments unavoidably affect others, often in deeply significant ways, would it not be responsible and a sign of genuine humanity to reflect on how consistently and how well we believe these judgments are being made by taking another look, for example, at how some people have been affected by our actions and how they or others will be affected if we continue acting in roughly the same or in some quite different way by new and self-conscious forethought?

Although consistency is a requisite to rationality, it is not a guarantee of correctness: certainly it is possible to be consistently inhumane, although difficult to persist in wrongdoing after becoming aware of being consistently inhumane. Be that as it may, I would appeal to the reader's own conception of what it means to live a dignified, humane life and ask whether it is not the case that one requisite of rationality is to be conscientious in trying to avoid moral tragedy.

What is a moral tragedy? I suppose to some extent moral tragedies have unique elements in them for every individual. Nevertheless, moral tragedy is something that can happen to any or all of us. A moral tragedy occurs when, after you have acted in a certain way and reflected on how you have acted, you come to the conclusion that, upon reflection, had you thought about it before you acted, you would have acted differently. There is a certain tragedy in that particular set of circumstances. Of course, it may not be your own reflection that most immediately makes you wish you had acted differently. The judgments, criticisms, disappointments, or sheer unhappiness of others may be the stimulus that causes you to think twice about how you have acted and how you will act in the future.

Whatever else ethics has to offer, its study does represent a modest but important means by which people can discover, before they act, how they would best like to act, and imaginatively test in advance some of the difficult choices that lie ahead. By doing this, students of ethics have the opportunity to acquaint themselves with their own deepest values and the way in which they tend to realize these values, and to try to bring their general modes of thinking, willing, and acting into line with those deepest values.

Of course, the study of ethics may also bring into question some of the values that are held by individuals or their cultures. Even then, ethics will provide ways of formulating and reformulating moral priorities, and will tend to separate what is ephemeral from what is more lasting and worthier of concerted commitment and effort.

A PREVIEW OF WHAT FOLLOWS

The remaining chapters of this book will take up the three kinds of questions with which we have said the study of ethics is concerned. Chapter 2 will describe the diverse inputs into policy decisions and will serve to illustrate how one may systematically think about and reflect upon a moral debate, whether with oneself or with others. Chapters 3 through 5 are concerned with an examination of normative ethics. In these chapters, we will frequently focus upon specific moral dilemmas that arise in the practice of medicine and in the attempt to cultivate professional conduct in medical practice; but each of these examples from medicine has broad applicability to our everyday lives as well, and to the kinds of decisions made by professionals other than health professionals.

In the final three chapters, we will take up relativism and metaethics. More specifically, we will try to indicate what the best thinking in ethics is about the extent to which moral judgments are like or unlike other kinds of knowledge and about the extent to which moral judgments do or do not have universal applicability and validity. Above all, in these last chapters, we will move toward indicating methods by which our moral judgments can be brought more clearly in line with our most cherished values, and methods by which we can generate rationally defensible inputs into our moral judgments and into the policies that guide our vocational and professional conduct.

In discussing these major questions of ethics and the answers being offered, I have endeavored to be fair in representing and presenting diverse points of view within ethics. At the same time, however, I argue for certain theories as being more plausible than others, so that this introduction to ethics is not a mere recitation of theories but a working effort to engage readers in debate about what is true and what is best. The present volume has a twofold purpose, then: to provide a preliminary review of the kinds of judgments that have issued from the discipline of ethics, and to invite you, the reader, to reflect upon and to reassess your own present judgments with respect to the questions of ethics and hence, at the same time, to reassess what you think is right and wrong, good and evil.

Chapter 1—Suggestions for Further Reading

Beach, Waldo, and Niebuhr, H. Richard, eds. *Christian Ethics*. 2d ed. New York: Ronald Press, 1973.

A widely used anthology of selections from the writings of major figures in Christian ethics. The introduction and the chapter on biblical ethics are distinct bonuses.

Brandt, Richard B. *Ethical Theory*. Englewood Cliffs, N.J.: Prentice-Hall, 1959.

Still the best and most comprehensive account of the major theories within contemporary moral philosophy. This is by no means an easy book.

Curran, Charles E. *Catholic Moral Theology and Dialogue*. Notre Dame, Ind.: Fides Publishers, 1972.

An innovative representation of contemporary trends.

Ford, John C., S.J., and Kelly, Gerald, S.J. *Contemporary Moral Theology,* vol. 1. Westminster, Maryland: The Newman Press, 1958.

A cautiously advanced version of pre–Vatican II thinking.

Forell, George W., ed. *Christian Social Teachings*. Garden City, N.Y.: Doubleday Anchor Books, 1966.

A very useful, quite comprehensive selection of readings in Christian social ethics. It includes biblical excerpts.

Fox, Marvin, ed. *Modern Jewish Ethics*. Columbus: Ohio State University Press, 1975.

An excellent, fairly comprehensive set of essays by contemporary Jewish ethicists, primarily concerned with the nature and scope of Jewish ethics.

Frankena, William K. *Ethics*. 2d. ed. Englewood Cliffs, N.J.: Prentice-Hall, 1973.

Perhaps the best brief yet fairly encompassing introduction to moral philosophy. It contains a very helpful short list of additional readings in moral philosophy.

Gustafson, James. "Christian Ethics." In *Religion* (Humanistic Scholarship in America: The Princeton Studies), edited by Paul Ramsey. Englewood Cliffs, N.J.: Prentice-Hall, 1965.

The best brief discussion of the themes and trends in contemporary Christian ethics.

Long, Edward LeRoy. *A Survey of Christian Ethics*. New York: Oxford University Press, 1967.

A fairly comprehensive overview of the major topics and positions in Christian ethics. A major bibliographical source.

Ramsey, Paul. *Basic Christian Ethics*. New York: Charles Scribner's Sons, 1950.

Continues to be one of the best introductions to Christian ethics in a short compass. Readers will be interested in the suggestions for further reading at the back of this book.

Reagan, George, C.M. *New Trends in Moral Theology: A Survey of Fundamental Moral Themes*. Paramus, N.J.: Paulist/Newman Press, 1971.

An overview and a rich bibliographical source focused on Roman Catholic works.

Taylor, Paul. *Principles of Ethics: An Introduction*. Encino, Calif.: Dickenson Publishing Co., 1975.

Noteworthy for the clarity of its exposition and for a rather substantial philosophical bibliography.

Williams, Bernard. *Morality: An Introduction to Ethics*. New York: Harper Torchbooks, 1972.

A lively account of some major theoretical quarrels in philosophical ethics.

chapter ii
ethics, policy, and population debates

Population growth is a widespread concern, much discussed in the media, in the schools, and in daily conversation. Environmental degradation, starvation, poverty, crowding, and unplanned pregnancies are among the serious problems that have been associated with population growth. These are problems that affect not only the decisions of policy-makers and a variety of professionals but the decisions of individuals and couples as well. For example, there are couples who say they do not plan to have any children because there are enough children in the world already. Regardless of whether the appeal to population growth in the world is the primary or sole reason such couples may have for deciding not to have children, and regardless of whether their decision is based on careful analysis, individuals or couples who seriously accept such a rationale for their decisions are assuming or acting exactly as if they have sufficient expertise in population matters as well as in ethics to feel that they "know" what is right or wrong. No one should be greatly surprised, then, if policy-makers and professionals who are neither specialists in population nor scholars in ethics feel that they also "know" what is right or wrong in the area of population policy and with respect to how many children they and others ought to have.

I would not claim that persons trained in ethics are any more qualified than other technical experts or other thoughtful persons to decide what is the very best population policy that any government or couple ought to pursue. But neither does the formulation of population policy flow directly and simply from analyses by population experts. In short, neither ethical nor social scientific expertise is sufficient by itself for ascertaining the best course to follow in population policy.

Of course, it may seem obvious to the reader that anyone suggesting or making policy in the population area will need to take account of what is known about population phenomena through the studies of demographers, sociologists, economists, psychologists, and other scholars. It may not be so readily apparent that moral reasoning, often implicitly, sometimes explicitly, influences individual and corporate formulations of the nature of population problems and population policy. By analyzing such moral reasoning and classifying alternatives where they exist, ethics can make a modest but definite contribution in providing a reasonable basis for deciding what problems count as population problems and what are the best policy responses aimed at alleviating such problems. This chapter intends to illustrate, at least in a preliminary way, how moral judgments and ethical theory enter into debates over population policy.

In describing and analyzing population-policy recommendations, we will be making use of the descriptive categories developed by Ralph Potter and briefly delineated in chapter 1. Each major point of view will be examined as to its empirical assumptions, quasi-theological beliefs, moral reasoning, and loyalties. Neither Potter nor I would claim that this mode of analysis is the only or even the most cogent way of assessing policy recommendations, but readers can judge its usefulness for themselves.

POPULATION-POLICY ALTERNATIVES[1]

Debates over the nature of population problems and the kinds of population policies that are needed to respond to these problems generate a great deal of heat. Deep differences of opinion are not in themselves surprising or disturbing when complex social problems and policies designed to alleviate them are under discussion. However, there is an especially urgent need to analyze population-policy debates, because of the serious nature of the disagreements that exist and the serious consequences either of choosing the wrong policies or of choosing none.

In this chapter, we will seek to describe as clearly as possible significant sources of agreement and disagreement about population policy. This will involve a description of three major groups whose population-policy recommendations vie for acceptance: (1) crisis environmentalists, (2) family planners, and (3) developmental distributivists. These three groups represent distinct policy orientations and priorities. The recommendations that are associated with these orientations are not mutually exclusive. For example, family planners may also favor policies being recommended by developmental distributivists. At the same time, there are family planners who are sympathetic to some of the analyses of crisis environmentalists. We are not concerned here with these overlapping allegiances, but, rather, with how these three distinct orientations within debates concerning population policy shape our understanding of population problems and with what responses to them are morally appropriate. After analyzing these views, we will briefly assess what appear to be the most cogent moral priorities for guiding population policy.

When we speak here of *policy recommendations,* we are referring to recommendations that specify a responsible agency, a goal, and appropriate means for its realization. In the population field, one can distinguish between population-influencing policies and population-responsive policies. Population-responsive policies are those that seek to ameliorate problems that arise as a consequence of population growth or population loss or problems associated with migration. Population-influencing policies are those that seek directly to influence populations to increase or decrease in number and/or to induce changes in location. In this essay our focus is on three different orientations toward what are considered to be population-influencing policies.

No attempt will be made to specify in advance what makes a policy a population policy nor what makes a problem a population problem. Delineations of population policy and population problems are at the very heart of the debates about population policy. As we shall see, each of these major groups under consideration defines population problems and population policies quite differently.

CRISIS ENVIRONMENTALISTS. Crisis environmentalists take the view that rapid population growth has already produced a serious crisis for the human species and the planet earth. Sometimes, as with Paul Ehrlich, the emphasis is on resource depletion, pollution, and environmental degradation.[2] Others, like William and Paul Paddock, concentrate more specifically on depletion of food resources and, in 1967, predicted widespread famine in 1975.[3] Garrett Hardin has stressed all of these themes as consequences of rapid population growth.[4] These four thinkers and those who share their viewpoint assume that population growth is likely to continue and even escalate in the absence of explicit governmental constraint or mutually agreed upon coercion. There is complete agreement that resources needed for the survival of the human species are finite and will be depleted unless population is held at a level that establishes a favorable balance between numbers of people and available resources.

Crisis Environmentalists: Empirical Assumptions. The key empirical assumption that characterizes crisis environmentalists is that as population increases, pollution, resource depletion, and environmental damage increase. Indeed, this group is virtually convinced that the number of people on the earth already exceeds the optimal level. The environmental threats to human survival are exacerbated, therefore, by every increase in the number of people, and the problems associated with these increases may, at any time, become irreversibly lethal because of the finite nature of the earth. Ehrlich expresses this in a very simple and clear formula: the environment is sick, the disease is overpopulation, the remedy is population control, using coercion as necessary.[5]

Crisis Environmentalists: Quasi-Theological Beliefs. It is not immediately evident that population density is the only or the most important factor in bringing about environmental degradation. Why, then, the reader may ask, do crisis environmentalists focus on overpopulation as the critical factor in environmental problems, and why also does coercion of a societal or governmental variety appear to be necessary? In Ehrlich's writings, it is implicitly assumed that economic interests and pollution on the part of large corporations are more difficult to change or control than individual fertility behavior. Even so, the interest that people take in having children is strong and may require governmental sanctions if birth rates are to be reduced. Kingsley Davis and Garrett Hardin have contended that there is no logical reason to expect individual couples to decide on an average family size that will be congruent with societal expectations or needs.[6] Davis based his argument largely on the discrepancy between family size desired and achieved, on the one hand, and the family-size norm necessary for approaching and achieving zero population growth. However, there is an assumption, explicitly articulated by Hardin, that the kind of self-interest that individuals invest in their children is such that the interest of the larger society in children is not and cannot be congruent with that of individuals. Hardin's argument bears scrutiny.

According to Hardin, childbearing can be compared with sheep raising. In his imaginative essay, he has the reader visualize a small group of sheepherders who share a common plot of ground for grazing. Each sheepherder desires to raise and nurture, for economic reasons, as many sheep as possible. Left to their own choices, individual sheepherders will increase their flocks to the point that the grazing land available will no longer sustain its ever-increasing use. To avoid this inevitable outcome, mutually agreed upon coercion is required. According to Hardin, the desire for children is comparable enough to the desire for more sheep to warrant the claim that as in the case of the sheepherders, individual couples will only be constrained at the level that societal survival demands by mutually agreed upon coercion. In a modern state, that means governmental intervention.

Crisis Environmentalists: Moral Reasoning. As Hardin's argument indicates, crisis environmentalists make the definite anthropological or even quasi-theological assumption that individual interests and societal interests are in a number of critical ways, and certainly in matters of procreation, in conflict with each other. Hence the need for coercion. Furthermore, the appeal to the finitude of the earth and its resources makes it seem self-evident that the moral argument for coercive population policies is justified because the very survival of the human species is at stake. This appeal to an ultimate threat to human life makes it understandable why there is very little discussion of questions of justice and liberty in the literature of crisis environmentalists, and that when there is mention of these moral values, they are easily swallowed up by appeals to the urgent necessity to avert ultimate disaster. The appeal to survival, therefore, is at the heart of the moral justifications that crisis environmentalists offer for coercive population policies. Some of the policies mentioned in this literature include economic incentives, both positive and negative;[7] compulsory abortion in certain cases;[8] triage in matters of food policy;[9] and antifertility chemicals in water supplies.[10]

Crisis Environmentalists: Loyalties. If one asks what loyalties are shared by crisis environmentalists, deep commitments to the continuation of all animal species and of the ecological systems that support life on this planet are very much in evidence. It is also true that many crisis environmentalists are biologists. (By no means are biologists as such necessarily crisis environmentalists:

some are definitely not.) Among other things, there is, therefore, an understandable conception of what kinds of things count as resources to be held precious and irreplaceable. Wilderness and other animal species are often singled out as such. Given these priorities, space becomes virtually as important a problem as environmental degradation by reason of industrial pollutants and the like. Even if consumption and pollution were greatly limited and altered in ways that would conserve resources, the sheer density of population would remain an issue with regard to how much wilderness and plant and animal species are to be preserved.[11] For this reason alone, crisis environmentalists would continue to speak of overpopulation as an immediate threat to the quality of life, if not to the survival of the human species, in spite of progress that does and may occur in pollution abatement and food production.

FAMILY PLANNERS. Although crisis environmentalists have received considerable publicity, certainly in this country, it is family planners who have had the ear of governments in the United States and in numerous countries throughout the world.[12] The family-planning movement in the United States has a history that can be traced to the work of Margaret Sanger and others who are founders of the family-planning movement in this country, a movement that has been exported all over the world by various planned parenthood organizations.[13] The thinking of family planners is well represented within the Report of the U. S. Commission on Population Growth and the American Future and within the official global policies of the Population Division of the U.S. Agency for International Development (USAID).[14] What, then, are the major tenets of family planners, and what are their specific objections to the views of crisis environmentalists?

Family Planners: Empirical Assumptions. Family planners, like crisis environmentalists, sometimes speak of overpopulation, but more often they focus upon unwanted fertility or rapid population growth. They have gathered data in many regions of the world which, on the face of it, lend support for the view that in every country and in most families, parents have children that they do not want; these data also allegedly indicate favorable attitudes toward the use of birth control methods. Family planners have concluded that if governments make birth control methods and the knowledge of their use readily and freely available to everyone, people would have fewer children.[15]

Sometimes family planners—particularly within the context of the Population Commission Report and the publications of USAID—amass arguments that are specifically designed to persuade people to have small families and to consider them ideal. Hence, such literature discusses the undesirability of large families: the larger the family, the more difficult it is to deal with poverty, to provide education for one's children, to accumulate savings for investments, and to maintain the health of mothers and of the children who might be born. All of these empirical claims argue that it is in the interest of each family to practice family planning and to stay small.

The Population Commission Report and USAID documents also stress the societal interest in curbing rapid population growth and in keeping the average family size small. In the words of the Population Commission Report:

> There is hardly any social problem confronting this nation whose solution would be easier if our population were larger. . . . After two years of concentrated effort, we have concluded that no substantial benefits would result from continued growth of the nation's population.
>
> The "population problem" is long run and requires long-run responses. It is not a simple problem. . . .
>
> It is a problem which can be interpreted in many ways. It is the pressure of population reaching out to occupy open spaces and bringing with it a deterioration of the environment. It can be viewed as the effect on natural resources of increased numbers of people in search of a higher standard of living. It is the impact of population fluctuations in both growth and distribution upon the orderly provision of public services. It can be seen as the concentration of people in metropolitan areas and depopulation elsewhere, with all that implies for the quality of life in both places. It is the instability over time of proportions of the young, the elderly, and the productive. For the family and the individual, it is the control over one's life with respect to the reproduction of new life—the formal and informal pronatalist pressures of an outmoded tradition, and the disadvantages of and to the children involved.[16]

The Population Commission set zero population growth as a desirable goal for the United States. Despite the alleged seriousness of population-related problems and a goal of zero population growth, however, family planners, unlike crisis environmentalists, do not recommend coercive government policies. On the contrary, they favor complete voluntarism in the form of government investment in free-standing birth control clinics to offer all the available methods of birth control to those who would not otherwise be able to afford them. The Population Commission proposed an expenditure of $1.8 million for the fiscal years 1974–78 inclusive for that purpose, more than 10 times as much as the $150 million it recommended for continuing the governmental provision of maternal and child health clinics.[17] In the light of their research on unwanted fertility, family planners expect individuals to use these governmental services for reducing family size and, hence, population growth in the United States and throughout the world.

Family Planners: Quasi-Theological Beliefs. There are two additional, significant reasons family planners do not advocate coercion and trust that governmental provision of birth control services will be efficacious in approaching zero population growth. The first is that family planners assume that there is no serious conflict between individuals and society, in that couples are expected to have fewer children and move in the direction of zero population growth. This strongly held assumption is partially supported by the data collected on unwanted fertility and on favorable attitudes toward the use of birth control methods. The belief that individual interests and societal interests will ultimately harmonize is completely at odds with the assumption of crisis environmentalists that such interests ultimately conflict. This difference provides one important rationale for the tendency of family planners to reject a crisis orientation.

Family Planners: Moral Reasoning. The second reason that family planners disavow coercion is that they put a strong value on freedom. Freedom for family planners largely means absence of governmental constraints. The Population Commission Report, in the chapter on resources and the environment, observes that

> population growth forces upon us slow but irreversible changes in life style. Imbedded in our traditions as to what constitutes the American way of life is freedom from public regulation—virtually free use of water; access to uncongested, unregulated roadways; freedom to do as we please with what we own; freedom from

permits, licenses, fees, red tape, and bureaucrats; and freedom to fish, swim, and camp where and when we will.[18]

In keeping with this view of freedom from regulation, the Population Commission and family planners generally advocate the removal of any existing impediments, including monetary costs, which would hinder anyone from access to abortion, sterilization, and contraceptive services.[19]

Family Planners: Loyalties. Family planners, as their name implies, began historically with a distinct loyalty to families. But increasingly, the family planning movement is focusing on the individual. In the Population Commission Report, it is definitely the individual and not the family whose welfare is of primary concern. The recommendations of the Population Commission to increase government expenditures for making birth control knowledge and methods freely available include specific recommendations to remove all barriers, legal or customary, that would prevent unmarried individuals and minors from receiving these same services. No individual is to be excluded from government subsidized birth control services, including sterilization and abortion, on the basis of age, marital status, or lack of consent from parents or other parties. Whereas, then, family planners used to focus on the welfare of families and the nation states in which they were found, now the focus is on individuals and their nation states. Global concern is present but not emphasized as it is in the crisis environmentalists.

DEVELOPMENTAL DISTRIBUTIVISTS. This group is characterized by its belief that certain kinds of improvements in socioeconomic conditions lead to lower birth rates as observed in the "demographic transition" experienced in Western countries. Although developmental distributivists include individuals and groups with a wide variety of religious and political affiliations, such as Roman Catholicism and Marxism, they are united in their opposition to the way in which crisis environmentalists and family planners depict the relationship between population growth and serious societal problems. The World Plan of Action forged at the Population Conference held at Bucharest in August, 1974, largely reflects the thinking and policies of developmental distributivists.[20]

Developmental Distributivists: Empirical Assumptions. To begin with, developmental distributivists have analyzed the complexity of the relationships between population variables and environmental problems. As Roger Revelle has noted:

> More than half of the environmental deterioration in the United States since 1940 . . . has resulted from our growing affluence and changes in consumption patterns—from our increasingly filthy habits. For example, one of the major sources of pollution is the growth of electric power generation from the burning of sulfur-containing coal and oil, which rose about fivefold between 1940 and 1965, while the population was growing by 47 percent. With the per capita power consumption of 1970, . . . our population would have to be reduced to 20 million souls to arrive at the same total power consumption as in 1940.[21]

The point of this analysis is that pollution and affluence grow much faster than the population and that pollution grows as affluence grows. If decreasing population growth will increase affluence, as many population experts assert, then decreasing population growth will increase environmental deterioration, unless of course our present modes of production, consumption, and waste disposal are changed. Developmental distributivists and others have argued, therefore, that our current habits and not population growth by itself are at the heart of those environmental problems that can be considered serious.

How do developmental distributivists view the availability of food and the problem of famine? One of the favorite examples of overpopulation according to crisis environmentalists is the country of India. There is, however, scholarly research on famines in India claiming that in the nineteenth century, famines were due to genuine food shortages but that in the twentieth century, famines are due to distribution problems and to the tendency for the price of food to rise sharply in periods of relative scarcity. In India, as in many economically developing countries, food production is increasing at a greater rate than population.[22] But poor people starve or are malnourished in India, as in other countries, because they do not always have the money or the knowledge to feed themselves properly. For example, a widely practiced feeding habit, withholding solid foods from infants in their first two years of life, is a major cause of infant mortality.[23] No reduction in population size and no reduction in family size will by itself affect this cause of malnutrition.

Revelle has calculated that it is technically possible to feed up to 38 to 48 billion people in this world, 10 to 13 times the present population.[24] He has also argued that the world has never had so much food and so small a proportion of starving people.[25] This is not to say that he or any other developmental distributivist is contending for a world of 30 to 40 billion people. The point is, rather, that people starve because of the policies their governments pursue, their poverty, and their lack of knowledge rather than because of a general lack of food or the lack of potential for producing it.

Whereas crisis environmentalists and family planners particularly stress the unfavorable socioeconomic consequences of large families and rapid population growth, developmental distributivists have seen unfavorable socioeconomic conditions as major factors in bringing about large families and rapid population growth. Developmental distributivists take the view that illiteracy, especially of women, high infant mortality rates, extremely unjust distributions of income, lack of governmental provision for the elderly, and underemployment and poor production in agriculture are among some of the most important socioeconomic conditions that contribute to high fertility rates and rapid population growth. These are precisely the causal links stressed in the World Plan of Action adopted at Bucharest.[26]

Developmental distributivists are not arguing that general improvements in socioeconomic conditions as measured by levels of per capita income or per capita gross national product will by themselves bring about lower fertility rates. The key to lowering fertility lies in the extensiveness of the distribution of income and of social services. After analyzing considerable data, William Rich concluded that

> development policies that focus on participation and increased access to benefits for the population as a whole do seem to produce a major impact on family size. In countries which have a relatively equitable distribution of health and education services, and which provide land, credit, and other income opportunities, the cumulative effect of such policies seems to be that the poorest half of the population is vastly better off than it is in countries with equal or higher levels of per capita GNP but poor distribution patterns. The combined effect of such policies has made it possible for some countries to reduce birth rates despite their relatively low levels of national production.[27]

Demographers have long theorized that the change to low birth rates in Western countries (the demographic transition) was associated with low infant mortality rates, high literacy rates, and processes of modernization that included such developments as higher income and better income distribution, improved agriculture, and provision for the elderly. Furthermore, there is evidence that the demographic transition that occurred in the more affluent countries of the West will also occur as a result of socioeconomic development in currently less affluent nations. Dudley Kirk's analysis concludes that a growing number of countries are entering a demographic transition at a somewhat faster rate than was true of Western countries.[28] Family planners have cited a number of countries that are experiencing significant declines in birth rates. They attribute these declines to the introduction of family-planning programs.[29] Developmental distributivists, however, examining the same data, point out that every one of these countries is experiencing important gains in distributing socioeconomic benefits and that it is precisely under these conditions that people use family-planning programs for the purpose of reducing birth rates.

Recently, Michael Teitelbaum has spoken of a new consensus that population policies should combine family-planning programs and socioeconomic development.[30] It should be recognized, however, that from the point of view of developmental distributivists, it is not just any kind of socioeconomic development, whether or not it is combined with family-planning programs, which will yield lower birth rates. Countries like Brazil and Mexico with much higher per capita income continue to have high birth and growth rates, whereas countries like Sri Lanka and Taiwan have had falling birth and growth rates with considerably lower levels of per capita income.[31] The difference lies in the type of socioeconomic development. Sri Lanka and Taiwan have raised the employment and income of the very poorest sectors of their societies and have greatly increased the distribution of income and social services as well. It should be noted also that where we do have controlled studies, family-planning programs by themselves have not proved efficacious in lowering birth rates. John Wyon, in a carefully controlled field study conducted in the Punjab area of India from 1953 to 1960, found that although a high proportion of couples could be induced to accept birth control methods, no appreciable change in birth rates resulted.[32] Johns Hopkins University did a similar study in Pakistan for five years with identical results.[33] In the late sixties, Wyon returned to the same villages in the Punjab which he had studied earlier. Now he found that birth rates were lower. Why? The most visible reason seemed to be that with the coming of the Green Revolution to that area, people there were experiencing higher income, more education, especially for girls, and fewer infant deaths.[34]

Developmental Distributivists: Quasi-Theological Beliefs. Developmental distributivists do agree with family planners that in procreative matters, it is reasonable to expect that the interests of individuals and couples will more or less correspond with the interests of their societies. However, unlike the family planners, developmental distributivists do not expect this to happen by itself or through policies that make all existing birth control methods and birth control information freely available to everyone. From the standpoint of developmental distributivists, the interests of individuals and of their societies can only be expected to harmonize when some reasonable degree of social justice has been realized. Developmental distributivists do not accept a notion of freedom that focuses exclusively on absence of constraint. If people are to be free, they must also have the ability and the means to make choices and to participate in the opportunities available within a given society. Having a small family, for example, makes sense if one can be relatively certain that one's children will have opportunities for health care, education, and future employment.

Developmental Distributivists: Moral Reasoning. Social justice as a requisite of population policy is the moral outlook characteristic of developmental distributivists. Marx, Engels, and subsequent Marxists rejected Malthus and subsequent Malthusians precisely in the name of social justice. At Bucharest, Marxists, Roman Catholics, and the great majority of representatives from various countries found themselves allied against the family planning ideology reflected in the views of the United States and its supporters.[35] What united these groups was the view that social justice in the form of better health care, better income distribution, better status for women, provision for the aged, and the like, constitute population policies. What is more, policies that strive to realize justice in these forms are not to be construed simply as responses to problems caused by population growth but are to be seen as policies that help to lower birth rates. It was not surprising, therefore, that crisis environmentalists did not even get a hearing at Bucharest.

Developmental Distributivists: Loyalties. Developmental distributivists represent a wide range of loyalties. Roman Catholics and others have a central focus on strengthening familial life. Marxists, of course, have a special interest in the working class. However diverse their other loyalties may be, developmental distributivists have a strong concern for human welfare on a global scale. Nothing less than regard for the fate of the whole human race unites them. All of these loyalties, however, are very much conditioned and shaped by strong national loyalties and interests.

AN ARGUMENT FOR JUSTICE AS A PRIORITY

What do we learn from the analysis of differing views of population problems and policy responses to them? There is no space here to do more than make some brief suggestions as to the direction in which I think the debate over population policy ought to go.

It should be evident that there is no clear agreement as to what are to be considered population-related problems, nor as to how serious these are. There is considerable consensus that environmental degradation is a serious matter, but the solutions to this problem require considerably more than changes in the numbers and concentrations of people. It is not difficult to make the point that the earth cannot sustain an indefinite number of people and that, therefore, there is a hypothetical condition that could be identified as "overpopulation." But there is not agreement as to how societies achieve and maintain zero population growth where this seems to be a reasonable goal for a given society.

To answer this kind of question, it is necessary to initiate and study population-influencing policies designed to solve some problem considered to be population related. One of the frustrations of the current analyses of family planning programs is that these programs do not, by and large, include sufficient data collection and the use of controls that would assist us in the debates over the successes and failures of these programs. Nor do we have any evidence, even if there were a consensus that serious social ills are population related, that the kinds of incentive programs and various forms of compulsion being suggested by some crisis environmentalists would actually work if they were adopted. No programs of this sort were recommended or even mentioned in the World Plan of Action forged at Bucharest.

A simple call for more research is not enough in this circumstance. The research most needed—namely, controlled study of population-influencing policies—is precisely under debate, and the evidence as to which of these policies is most efficacious and most feasible would only be known once a number of them were tried. How, then, does one choose the social experiments that will deal with some of the serious problems that are thought to be population related? It seems to me that the decision should rest on strictly moral grounds.

At this very point, crisis environmentalists would tend to object. What is characteristic of crisis environmentalists is the view that population-related problems have put us into an immediate crisis and threaten what is surely the most basic moral value on which all of us would agree, namely, the value of life itself and the survival of the whole human species. Now I agree that the value of life is fundamental and will assume that readers and the other population orientations share the desire to secure as far as is humanly possible the survival of the human species. But is it population growth as such that poses an immediate threat to human survival?

Although there is considerable debate about the imminence of serious, even irreversible threats to the ecosphere, it is clear that constraints on our wastefulness and pollution will need to become part of modern industrial life. Scientists contribute to human welfare and survival by documenting these necessities and constraints. However, crisis environmentalists have done us a disservice by giving us simplified, even factually false accounts of the way in which population and environmental variables interact. Indeed, some scientists like Ehrlich and Ehrlich have made astounding factual errors in their calculations of strains on our environment. A number of these have been documented by Revelle, such as miscalculations of how long it will take for silt to fill Lake Nasser, misstatements of the need for water in the United

States, errors in estimating annual fish production, large overstatements of the existence of DDT in the environment, et cetera.[36] If biologists and other scientists of the environment are to have credibility with the public, with their peers, and with political decision-makers, they will have to maintain the high standards of science in what is admittedly an area in which values other than truth-telling and precision are creeping to the fore. J. Bronowski states "the scientist's moral" as one that brooks "no distinction between ends and means." He clearly sees this as the practice of scientists and cites with approval this description of scientific practice and morality:

> In like manner, if I let myself believe anything on insufficient evidence, there may be no great harm done by the mere belief; it may be true after all, or I may never have occasion to exhibit it in outward acts. But I cannot help doing this great wrong towards Man, that I make myself credulous. The danger to society is not merely that it should believe wrong things, though that is great enough; but that it should become credulous.[37]

Garrett Hardin is another crisis environmentalist who has strained the usual limits of credibility.[38] There is no need in the present essay to repeat and elaborate the very cogent arguments by Murdoch and Oaten directed against the use by Hardin of the lifeboat metaphor.[39] The crux of the matter is that we are hardly in a lifeboat situation with respect to population-related problems. As Murdoch and Oaten pointed out, taking a lifeboat stance at this time for the United States would not only be politically detrimental, it would also worsen the current situation of some nations and would actually, so far as our best evidence indicates, contribute to maintaining high birth rates by exacerbating conditions of poverty. It should be noted also that environmental scientists are going to have to become much clearer about whether they really mean to argue as though environmental resources are finite and nonrenewable. Limiting population growth in any given generation is not nearly so important an issue if the basic necessities of human existence are finite and nonrenewable. If we do have enough renewable resources to keep the human species viable for a great number of subsequent generations, then it is of course important to consider our responsibilities over many generations. Furthermore, the exhaustion of certain finite and nonrenewable resources becomes a matter of the loss of a particular pattern of consumption or life-style and not a matter of life or death for the species where the basic necessities of life are seen as renewable.

Family planners have stressed the value of freedom in the form of absence of constraint. They have collected data that lend credence to the possibility of maintaining voluntarism in population policy. I have no quarrel with this aim and the value that propels it. However, family-planning programs and the moral basis on which they are predicated are inadequate.

Consider certain insufficiencies in the moral basis of current family-planning policies of the United States. On the face of it, these policies would seem to be beneficial; and to some degree, where they meet definite needs, they are. But family planners have not given ample attention to the special conditions associated with poverty that make the free availability of birth control methods something less than a clear benefit. As developmental distributivists have indicated, there are many circumstances under which the poor need children for labor and for security in old age. Also, it is the poor who will lose some of their children through disease and malnutrition. These conditions of poverty are not eliminated by having small families. As one poverty-stricken mother has eloquently put it:

> Even without children my life would still be bad—they're not going to give us what *they* have, the birth control people. They just want us to be a poor version of them, only without our children and our faith in God and our tasty fried food, or anything.[40]

It can be argued, therefore, that the provision of birth control techniques and knowledge for the poor without changing their circumstances in any other respect may fail to improve, or may even worsen, their situation. Is such a policy, then, a violation of justice?

From a certain utilitarian perspective, one could argue that justice will have been obtained if family-planning policies serve to bring about the greatest good for the greatest number, even though some of those who are least well off in the society may not directly benefit. But even if family-planning policies were efficacious in lowering birth rates, the fact that for some these policies were disadvantageous could be construed as a violation of the basic principles of justice. As the philosopher John Rawls has argued, the fairness of a policy depends on whether at least in part the implementation of that policy is advantageous to everyone, not simply the greatest number of persons affected by the policy.[41]

Applying Rawls's theory of justice, a policy that seeks to be advantageous for society as a whole through reducing its population growth will only be a just policy to the extent that it is advantageous to every member of that society and not simply advantageous for the greatest number or for the society as a whole. Even if, therefore, the government provision of freestanding birth control clinics to serve the poor, who could not otherwise afford them, were to achieve some social benefit for the majority of a society, it would on this principle be unjust because it is not clearly advantageous to the poor unless something else is done to assure a better life for poor people who reduce their family size. Among the unemployed, where their unemployment is not eliminated or adequately compensated and yet aid to dependent children is provided, there is no predictable advantage to childlessness. This is exactly one reason blacks in the United States have seen genocidal overtones in government sponsorship of freestanding birth control clinics. And as we have indicated before, in a number of circumstances, as in subsistence agriculture, children are clearly economic assets, not liabilities, even on economic grounds.

This is not to argue against the provision of family-planning services. Maternal and child health clinics in the United States have provided such services, and the poor have in this context requested such services. When contraceptive services are accompanied by maternal and child health services, they begin to create the conditions under which the poor see some hope that their children will live and that the government is concerned with their present and future welfare. Contraceptive services without facilities for reducing infant and maternal deaths provide little basis for such a hope, certainly not from the perspective of the poor.

From the standpoint of justice, and also from the standpoint of what appear to be population-related variables, the following types of policies suggested at Bucharest deserve a chance in countries that are concerned about population growth as well as in countries where these policies have not as yet been implemented to any significant degree:

1) good health services available to all, including contraceptive services in the context of providing care for the whole family;

2) literacy and nutritional education, especially for women, where there are inequalities in this respect (This policy along with the policy above would have the effect of reducing infant and maternal mortality);

3) labor intensive development, particularly in the agricultural sphere;

4) equality for women;

5) governmental programs that provide for the aged in ways that do not make them dependent upon the survival and prosperity of their children;

6) improvements in the distribution of income and income-earning opportunities.

Each one of these policies is in itself advantageous to those who are now disadvantaged. Each one of them is also potentially a population-influencing policy in the direction of lowering birth rates. Each and every one of these has its own moral justification, although the specific form this would take is subject to debate and would need to be elaborated. The extent to which any or all of these can be implemented will, of course, depend upon the resources available to any government that seeks to do so.

What I have tried to argue in only a preliminary and suggestive way is that these policies have relevance to what are considered to be population-related issues, and at the same time are ingredients in the realization of social justice by providing advantages to the relatively disadvantaged. There is no decisive evidence that they will or will not work as population policies. There is evidence, however, that the notion of justice implicit in them is one which the large bulk of the world's population clearly understands and endorses. And as the discussion above has suggested, such policies may be more morally justified than others.

Adequate bases for the notion of justice and the mode of moral reasoning I have been employing in this chapter have not been provided as yet. Subsequent chapters will more fully discuss such normative and metaethical considerations. This is not to say that readers will then be convinced of the viewpoint being espoused here, but rather that they will have been offered a more complete basis for forming a judgment.

Chapter II—Suggestions for Further Reading

Berelson, Bernard. "Beyond Family Planning," *Studies in Family Planning,* no. 38. New York: The Population Council. February, 1969.

A very comprehensive discussion of population-policy suggestions and an excellent bibliographical resource in this area. The author favors family planning as a policy.

————. "The Great Debate on Population Policy: An Instructive Entertainment." An occasional paper of the Population Council, 1975. As its subtitle promises, an entertaining dialogue among the major policy protagonists. As in his earlier essay, Berelson is an inveterate family planner. An excellent update of significant bibliographical references.

Callahan, Daniel, ed. *The American Population Debate.* Garden City, N.Y.: Doubleday & Co., 1971.

A very readable anthology that introduces the reader to the wide-ranging nature of debates regarding population problems, in this instance with respect to the United States.

Green, Ronald M. *Population Growth and Justice: An Examination of Moral Issues Raised by Rapid Population Growth.* Harvard Dissertations in Religion, 5. Missoula, Montana: Scholars Press, *1976.*

The author uses John Rawls's theory of justice to clarify and assess views of distributive justice that underlie various attempts to understand and cope with population growth. A helpful bibliography is appended.

Veatch, Robert M., ed. *Population Policy and Ethics: The American Tradition.* New York: Irvington Press, 1977.

A number of essays, all focused on ethical issues. This volume includes a discussion of Jewish, Protestant, and Roman Catholic views on population-policy–related matters and a considerable number of references for further study.

chapter iii
normative ethics

In our previous chapter, we noted that decisions regarding the rightness or wrongness of specific actions or policies cannot be simply deduced from or based upon situational analyses provided by the natural and social sciences. A portion of any debate concerning what is right or wrong involves some implicit or explicit mode of moral reasoning. Ethics, both normative and metaethical, with its explicit concern to engage in moral reasoning and to render it more precise, has, therefore, like the natural and social sciences, a distinct though limited contribution to make to actual decision-making, to understanding some of the reasons for conflicting points of view regarding what is right or wrong. Just as we cannot make the correct moral decision if our facts are inaccurate or incomplete, so we cannot make the correct policy decision if our moral reasoning is faulty or unreasonable.

Normative ethics and metaethics are both concerned to provide an understanding of moral reasoning. For normative ethics, the task is to identify moral standards and the type of reasoning about moral standards that provides the most plausible understanding of what these standards are. For metaethics, the task is to discover and delineate the extent to which our particular moral judgments are reasonable or otherwise justifiable, and to specify in what sense and to what degree normative ethics is a source of relatively reliable knowledge, useful to all of us, whether making individual decisions or decisions regarding public policy. In this and the subsequent two chapters, we will describe and exemplify normative ethics. Our discussions of metaethical issues are reserved for chapters 6, 7, and 8.

MORAL PRINCIPLES AS CONSTITUTIVE RULES

In his remarkable little book *Christian Morals Today,* Bishop John Robinson took special pains to depict Christian ethics as modern, and certainly nonlegalistic, in its outlook. He assured Christians that they should not have a troubled conscience about the different moral perspectives and judgments exhibited by Christians over time and across contending groups and pleaded with them not to "fear, flux, or be alarmed at the relativity of all ethics to the ethos of their day." Curiously enough, however, he felt compelled to qualify these observations in the following way:

> I would, of course, be the first to agree that there are a whole class of actions—like stealing, lying, killing, . . . which are so fundamentally destructive of human relationships that no differences of century or society can change their character.[1]

This claim by Bishop Robinson introduces the normative question—namely, the question as to whether and in what form there are right- and wrong-making characteristics of actions and policies that have some claim to recognition as such over time and across cultures. Quite literally, ethics is the study of ethos; and normative ethics is the attempt to find some moral rule or set of moral rules that, though part of an ethos, are not limited to it, having a much more enduring and basic form than other constantly changing judgments, policies, and rules.

The psychologist Jean Piaget recognized these two different kinds of rules when he made the distinction between what he called constitutive rules and constituted rules. Constitutive rules are requisite to the very processes of formulating or deciding upon rules. If, for example, one is trying to decide the rules of a game, one presupposes that persons will speak the truth to others and that agreements will take on the form of a promise to abide by the rules that are decided upon. Also, the rules of any game will presuppose some notion of fairness—that is, the rules will apply equally to persons in similar situations as specified within the context of the rules of the game as constituted. Rules of fairness, truth-telling, and promise-keeping, therefore, are seen as constitutive—that is, as requisites for the very process of deciding the nature of rules or laws that are to govern interpersonal interaction and social institutions. As a variant of Bishop Robinson's formulation, we might say that lying, breaking promises, and unfair procedures would be destructive of the human relationships that are endemic to the formulation and acceptance of any standards, laws, and procedures needed for cooperative behavior in community, and that all communities recognize, implicitly or explicitly, their general wrong-making character.

One of the main enterprises of ethics has been precisely the effort to conceptualize the nature and number of these constitutive rules. Drawing upon the analogy used in chapter 1, we can say that just as scientists have looked at the basic elements out of which nature is composed and can be composed, ethicists have sought the constitutive rules or elements out of which other rules and laws are, can be, and ought to be composed. And the identification of constitutive rules in ethics has the same potential value or function as the identification of basic elements of nature in science. It allows people to benefit from the past by giving them the kind of knowledge that makes it possible to assess more accurately the impact of human decisions. Constitutive rules can serve to guide rule- and law-making in the social sphere just as the basic elements of nature can serve to guide the manufacture of material products.

What we have been calling constitutive rules is a somewhat more precise way of referring to what in ethics are more usually called moral principles. Henceforth we shall use the term *moral principles* and shall consider it a synonym for *constitutive rules* as described above.

UTILITARIANISM

Our discussion of normative ethics begins with utilitarian theory, because of its considerable immediate intellectual appeal to the contemporary mind. Scientific theories that can analyze things into their simplest and most basic constitutive elements have always earned our utmost respect. Note, for example, the tremendous prestige and influence of atomic theory that analyzes all matter whatsoever into one basic, constitutive element and continues to break that element down even further into nucleii, and so forth. In an analogous way, the utilitarians have sought one single moral principle by means of which all rules and laws could and ought to be formulated.

As in atomic physics, there are some apparent advantages that accrue from identifying and specifying a single moral principle constitutive of all moral judgments. At least three such advantages were specifically claimed by John Stuart Mill and echoed in the work of contemporary utilitarians: it would resolve conflicts among rules and the problem of exceptions to rules, it would improve our understanding of love and justice and resolve the apparent conflict between them, and it would provide a moral rule, namely, a moral principle, that can be stated in an exceptionless form.[2]

Although Bentham is his mentor and intellectual predecessor in giving utilitarianism its modern form, Mill is undoubtedly the intellectual champion and sustenance for contemporary utilitarianism.[3] He took the view that the rightness or wrongness of any action is decided by its consequences, more specifically, by whether its consequences are best on the whole. His particular understanding of what is best on the whole was that which brings about the most happiness or the least suffering, i.e., the best balance of pleasure over pain for the greatest number.

By using this formula as the one moral principle by means of which rightness and wrongness are identified and judged, utilitarians claim that conflicting rules can be adjudicated and exceptions to rules decided. Indeed, modern economics has picked up a variant of this utilitarian formula because of the way in which it allows for the quantification of welfare. Cost/benefit analyses make quantified judgments about the most favorable balance of benefits over harms that any particular economic policy will bring about.

A second advantage that utilitarianism is alleged to offer lies in its understanding of the relation between love and justice. On Mill's view, the Judeo-Christian obligation to love one's neighbor is best understood and fulfilled when decisions regarding the welfare of our neighbors are decided by a rational calculation of what action will bring about the greatest happiness for the greatest number. On this analysis, utility, as the moral principle by which the rightness and wrongness of all actions are to be judged, offers the best understanding of the obligation to love one's neighbor.

> In the golden rule of Jesus of Nazareth, we read the complete spirit of the ethics of utility. To do as you would be done by, and to love your neighbor as yourself, constitute the ideal perfection of utilitarian morality.[4]

Having incorporated love as a moral obligation into his utilitarian formula, Mill adds the further claim that justice is not an additional moral principle. Justice, like love, can be understood as an obligation to realize the best consequences on the whole, i.e., the greatest happiness for the greatest number.

Mill argues that justice as a form of equity is never perfectly realized.[5] In every human situation and in every society, decisions about equity are really based on approximations of whatever is judged as bringing about the greatest happiness for the greatest number. Judging the extent to which both love and justice are being realized in this world is a judgment about the extent to which utility, according to Mill's formula, is being implemented. So far as moral priorities are concerned, therefore, there is only one: utility. Love and justice may appear to be distinct, additional, moral principles, but on further analysis, there is nothing about them that is morally right or wrong except insofar as they contribute to or hinder the realization of the greatest happiness for the greatest number.

In Christian ethics, Joseph Fletcher has taken precisely Mill's view of justice and the relationship between utility and justice:

> Justice is nothing other than love working out its problems. . . .
> Justice is love coping with situations where distribution is called for.
> . . . As the love ethic searches seriously for a social policy it must
> form a coalition with utilitarianism. It takes over from Bentham and
> Mill the strategic principle of "the greatest good of the greatest
> number." . . . In the coalition the hedonistic calculus becomes the
> agapeic calculus, the greatest amount of neighbor welfare for the
> largest number of neighbors possible.[6]

For Fletcher, then, love and justice are the same, and "love only is always good." Love is the one moral rule that can be stated in an exceptionless form. To determine whether an act is loving or just is to ask whether it satisfies the utilitarian calculus. And according to Fletcher, "If love does not calculate both the immediate and the remote consequence of its decisions, it turns selfish, childish, soft, subverting its own limitless, all-embracing work."[7] Thus, by putting equal weight on immediate as well as remote consequences, the coalition with Bentham and Mill is complete. In effect, then, the utilitarian calculus, which Fletcher calls love, becomes the one exceptionless moral rule.

Christian ethics has long puzzled over the relationship between love and justice. In equating them and joining them to the utilitarian calculus, Fletcher sees himself as cutting this burdensome, unnecessary Gordion knot.

The third advantage claimed by utilitarianism follows from what has already been said. The utilitarians, including Bentham,

Mill, and Fletcher, are convinced that they have found the one moral and rationally calculable standard by means of which the morality of all institutions and practices as well as all personal and interpersonal decisions can and ought to be judged. All moral rules except this one moral principle expressed by the utilitarian calculus are rules that have exceptions and/or come into conflict with one another. Only the utilitarian formula can be stated in an exceptionless form: it is always *the* moral standard by which every decision about what is right or wrong, good or bad, is and ought to be decided. It is a universally recognizable and universally binding moral rule. It is the one constitutive rule or moral principle found within the ethos of the moral life. There are no other candidates.

MORAL PROBLEMS FOR UTILITARIANS

Utilitarian thinking as represented in Mill's work is quite pervasive in our time. Certainly there are many instances of it in the decisions and literature of the medical and legal professions. Of course, it is not always pleasure that is evoked as the greatest good for the greatest number. Sometimes it is the public interest, sometimes it is money. Very often in medicine, it is the risk-benefit ratio that provides a basis for deciding what is right or wrong. Very often, also, certain risks to human beings are alleged to be justified on the grounds that risks on the part of the few now will eventuate into great benefits for the many in the future. In short, the kind of thinking Mill developed is very much a part of the contemporary ethos represented in the professions.

The high value that we place on quantitative types of thinking makes it appear that Mill has certainly given us a more precise rendition than any previous ethical theories of how to decide what constitutes love and justice. Any theory that provides a clearer picture of the basis on which we can call an act compassionate or just has an immediate practical appeal. But does Mill's theory actually help us in this way? In what follows, I shall argue that it does not. On the contrary, Mill's form of utilitarianism creates practical moral difficulties and dilemmas that greatly complicate our moral decisions and may lead us to follow policies quite out of harmony with our own most deeply held values.

One of the most attractive features of Mill's type of theory is that it reduces to one the number of morally significant relationships in which any of us stands in relation to others, namely, that of benefiting others. The basis for deciding that an act is right is that it is expected to produce the best balance of pleasure over pain or the greatest happiness for the greatest number. But let us consider, for a moment, the application of utilitarian thinking to the relationship between physicians and patients.

If one asks from the standpoint of Mill's utilitarianism who it is that physicians should treat, the answer to that question, presumably, is those who stand to benefit most and those who, when benefited, will contribute most to the greatest amount of benefit on the whole. Using this kind of reasoning as a guide, one could very well argue that physicians waste far too much time on extremely ill patients, many of whom have a risk of dying. From the cost-benefit point of view implied by the utilitarian formula, people who are not very ill and who respond quickly to medication or various forms of minor surgery would cost less and benefit more from medical care than people with advanced cancer, failing kidneys, or the like. It is clear, then, which patients would receive the higher priority if it is the greatest happiness of the greatest number that one is thinking about as one considers these cases.

Consistent application of the utilitarian formula, on the basis of which one allocates the time and skills of professionals, runs counter to those moral sensitivities that at present guide physicians to put those who are critically ill ahead of those whose illnesses are not life threatening. It would be considered quite unfair in the general course of practicing medicine to give no special priority to those who will die without medical assistance, and it would surely be considered even more unfair to put dying patients at the bottom of the list of those who should receive medical assistance. The utilitarian formula, then, is in certain instances quite out of harmony with our moral sensitivities regarding what should have weight in our decisions and policies. In the practice of medicine, each person does not have the same priority. Whether someone will receive medical treatment and how soon, will depend in large part upon strictly medically defined needs and estimates of the extent to which the very survival of the patient is at stake.

Consider another kind of example. A general practitioner in Kansas once told an astonished audience of college students that 75 percent of his patients really had no physical ailments, none that required the kind of medical intervention that he had been trained to give. Yet they were his patients. On what grounds? Though he did not raise this question, presumably he believed that he could be of some benefit. Administering placebos, for example, can be beneficial. You can give people placebos, and they will feel better. From a strictly utilitarian perspective, there is nothing wrong with that. Indeed, there are even strong reasons for doing precisely that to increase the general happiness in a simple, harmless way.

So here we see a situation in which the physician stands to benefit someone else, and on that basis, people who have no physical illness may become and remain patients. But one could ask another kind of question. When people go to a physician to be diagnosed for some symptom, are they not entitled to be told truthfully that they are free of any physical ailment? Furthermore, are they not also entitled to expect that physicians will acknowledge the limits of their own art, namely, that if the physician has no diagnosis for the symptom, the patients will be told this so that they may choose for themselves what other steps would be appropriate to deal with the symptoms that are beyond the knowledge of a physician?

We are not debating here the relative merits and liabilities of using placebos under certain circumstances. We are simply illustrating a type of situation in which we can see that the relationship of physicians to their patients is not only one of potentially or actually benefiting them but also one of telling them the truth and of exhibiting a special concern for saving their lives insofar as the interventions of medicine are efficacious for that purpose. Mill's utilitarian formula, therefore, if used as the *sole* basis for practicing medicine, could provide a justification for massive deceit as well as for unjust forms of discrimination among persons seeking help. The physician-patient relation cannot be morally justified simply on the basis that some good comes of it. Physicians, too, have promises to keep and commitments to honor, and it would be considered a grave breach of ethics to adopt as a working policy the attitude that one's patients ought to be risked, sacrificed, or abandoned wherever by doing so a greater good can be accomplished.

There is another serious problem with utilitarianism in all its forms that deserves our attention. According to the utilitarian, the rightness or wrongness of actions or policies depends upon what will follow from carrying out that action or policy. In short, only the future counts with respect to what is morally significant, and not the past. The rightness and wrongness of acts and policies are judged solely in terms of their consequences. Why is this problematic? Let us consider, for a moment, the example found in Joseph Fletcher's *Situation Ethics,* which since the first time I read it has never ceased to stand out in my mind. Fletcher has us imagine a situation in which only one of two persons can be rescued from a burning building. We know that one of these is a medical genius; the other is one of our parents. For Fletcher, it is obvious that you rescue the genius and not your parent. Some people believe, however, that it is obviously right to rescue one's parent, especially when nothing further is known about the medical genius.

Underlying this disagreement as to what is obvious are two very different ways of thinking about the right- and wrong-making characteristics of actions and policies. Fletcher is looking at the greatest good for the greatest number that could result from rescuing the medical genius. If he were thinking not only about the future but also about the past—for example, the fact that his parent was responsible for making his life possible at all—the rightness of rescuing the genius would not be so self-evident. After all, the moral basis for saving the life of one's parent is certain. You know that your parent has done something for you, and that is the source of a bond that theories other than utilitarianism have recognized as morally significant. Gratitude for past benefits might provide a sufficient moral basis for rescuing one's parent. At the very least, it would certainly make one question the "obvious" rightness of bypassing one's parent for the medical genius.

Fletcher assumes, as do other utilitarians, that it is somehow rational to consider future consequences even though they are quite hypothetical. Indeed, as we noted before, Bentham and Mill argued that the more remote consequences were to be considered equally with the more immediate and that it was rational to do so.

Yet, is it not possible that the medical genius might be one who will resurrect and successfully conduct germ warfare, that he might be a successor to Hitler or Stalin or some such source of evil on a large scale? Though we cannot say exactly what kinds of things our parent will do if rescued, we shall probably be able to make more nearly accurate predictions in this particular instance than in the case of the medical genius. In any event, why should probable benefits, which if unfulfilled or miscalculated would make the action wrong, count more or, as Fletcher would have it, be treated as absolutely determinative? Certainly the possibility of expressing gratitude or of otherwise maintaining a bond between persons is a weighty consideration. In the case of a parent, one of the past grounds for gratitude is a particularly precious and morally significant gift, namely, life itself.

FORMALISM: AN ALTERNATIVE TO UTILITARIANISM

Because of these very moral problems or paradoxes that it generates, utilitarianism has not gone unchallenged. Indeed, utilitarianism does not appear to be the dominant viewpoint within philosophical and religious ethics today. One of the most influential challenges to utilitarianism has come from the pen of Sir W. David Ross.[8] The impact of his critique in philosophical circles has been enormous.

With characteristic delicacy and precision, Ross does not begin his attack on utilitarianism until he has clarified the form in which the theory is most attractive. He notes that the philosopher G. E. Moore, writing at the turn of the twentieth century, did not share with his predecessors Bentham and Mill the claim that pleasure alone is good, and pain evil. For Moore, the one moral principle by means of which to judge what is right is best described in the formula "productive of the greatest good" and not in the more restrictive formula of Bentham and Mill, that is, "productive of the greatest pleasure." Ross argues that Moore's formulation of the utilitarian principle is more plausible because "on reflection it seems clear that pleasure is not the only thing in life that we think good in itself, that for instance we think the possession of a good character, or an intelligent understanding of the world, as good or better."[9] Furthermore, as Ross rightly contends, since Mill, like Moore, assumes as the basis for his theory that whatever produces the maximum good is right, both theories will have been refuted if one can show that productivity of the maximum good is not what makes all right actions right. (It goes without saying that Bentham and Fletcher would also be refuted if Mill and Moore can be proved wrong.)

Ross launches his critique of utilitarianism with an appeal to our ordinary moral sensitivities.

> When a plain man fulfills a promise because he thinks he ought to do so, it seems clear that he does so with no thought of its total consequences, still less with any opinion that these are likely to be the best possible. He thinks in fact much more of the past than of the future. What makes him think it right to act in a certain way is the fact that he has promised to do so—that and, usually, nothing more.[10]

He notes that utilitarian theory draws much of its sustenance from a consideration of exceptional cases in which, as Ross says, "the consequences of fulfilling a promise (for instance) would be so disastrous to others that we judge it right not to do so." Ross readily concedes that such cases exist and that, for example, he would certainly break a promise, made for trivial reasons, to a friend, if by so doing he could "prevent a serious accident or bring relief to the victims of one." Utilitarians believe that the reason for breaking such a promise is precisely in order to bring into existence more good by the one action than by the other. Ross, however, claims that a different account may be given of such an example. People recognize not only fulfilling promises but also preventing injury and relieving distress as moral principles. In a situation that involves keeping a promise as well as preventing serious injury or relieving serious distress, we try to ascertain which of these right-making characteristics is the one, under the circumstances, that is most stringent.

Ross buttresses his view that the rightness of our actions does not depend solely on how much good they produce or evil they prevent by arguing that if "I could bring equal amounts of good into being by fulfilling my promise and by helping some one to whom I had made no promise, I should not hesitate to regard the former as my duty."[11] Similarly, physicians would not consider it right to abandon patients to whom they are already committed in order to confer an equal benefit or treatment on someone else to whom no promises to provide treatment had been made. Yet, as

Ross notes, if one takes the view that what is right is right solely because it is productive of the most good, promises and commitments would provide no basis for thinking that there is any difference in the rightness of two acts that would bring about equal amounts of good. Indeed, there would be no basis on which to consider one more obligatory than the other.

Utilitarians would have us resolve conflicts among competing moral claims by deciding which action or policy among the alternatives would produce the most good. As we noted, therefore, utilitarians are asserting that there is only one morally significant relation in which our neighbors stand to each of us, namely, being actual or possible beneficiaries of our actions. Ross agrees that our neighbors are related to us in this way and that this relation is morally significant. But, says Ross, our neighbors may also be related to us as promisee to promisor, creditor to debtor, wife to husband, child to parent, friend to friend, et cetera, and each of these relations is the foundation of a moral claim "which is more or less incumbent on me according to the circumstances of the case." This, Ross argues, is the situation in which we usually find ourselves, one in which we are confronted by more than one moral claim or moral principle and in which we must make a decision as to which of these principles is the one upon which we are to act.[12]

With considerable courage, Ross is prepared to confront the sharply honed critical faculties of his philosophical colleagues with the following list of right- and wrong-making characteristics of actions or policies, a list of moral principles that neither Ross nor I would consider complete, final, or perfectly stated:

(1) Some duties rest on previous acts of my own. These duties seem to include two kinds, (a) those resting on a promise or what may fairly be called an implicit promise, such as the implicit undertaking not to tell lies which seems to be implied in the act of entering into conversation (at any rate by civilized men), or of writing books that purport to be history and not fiction. These may be called the duties of fidelity. (b) Those resting on a previous wrongful act. These may be called the duties of reparation. (2) Some rest on previous acts of other men, i.e. services done by them to me. These may be loosely described as the duties of gratitude. (3) Some rest on the fact or possibility of a distribution of pleasure or happiness (or of the means thereto) which is not in accordance with the merit of the persons concerned; in such cases there arises a duty to upset or prevent such a distribution. These are the duties of justice. (4) Some rest on the

mere fact that there are other beings in the world whose condition we can make better in respect of virtue, or of intelligence, or of pleasure. These are the duties of beneficence. (5) Some rest on the fact that we can improve our own condition in respect of virtue or of intelligence. These are the duties of self-improvement. (6) I think that we should distinguish from (4) the duties that may be summed up under the title of ''not injuring others.'' No doubt to injure others is incidentally to fail to do them good; but it seems to me clear that non-maleficence is apprehended as a duty distinct from that of beneficence, and as a duty of a more stringent character.[13]

Ross notes two objections that utilitarians might raise against this list. First, they might argue that there are some problems in being certain that this list is correct or complete. But as Ross points out, utilitarians have the same problem with respect to identifying what is good or putting forth a list of goods by means of which they will judge which actions are productive of the greatest good. How can one be certain that such a list, too, is correct or complete? This question is one that will occupy us in our final two chapters where we will look at the basis on which our moral judgments may be ''corrected'' or rendered more or less rational. Second, utilitarians claim that Ross's list does not provide a sure way of choosing among conflicting duties, whereas their formula does. But does it really? Utilitarians must face the same difficulty in deciding which action is right in a particular case whenever a particular action can be seen as productive of more than one thing that is good or when two or more actions can be seen as productive of good.

It is precisely these difficulties in the application of the utilitarian formula that prompted Bentham and Mill to seek the *one* good thing in itself by means of which to judge the rightness and wrongness of actions. If there is only one thing that is good, then to decide what is right is to decide which action brings about the greatest degree of that one thing that is good. If this be pleasure, as it was for Bentham and Mill, it means calculating the greatest amount of pleasure as well as the least amount of pain for the greatest number of persons.

Moore and subsequent utilitarians have not been content to consider pleasure the only good. Ross's argument against Bentham and Mill, as well as these later utilitarians, is that bringing about the maximum amount of good is not the only right-making characteristic of actions, regardless of whether good is seen as pleasure or as involving goods in addition to or instead of pleasure. At the very least, there are relationships to the past that are morally significant, such as having made a promise, having wronged someone, and having been benefited. What good may result from keeping promises, making up for past wrongs, and showing gratitude is not the only moral ground for thinking that in specific instances, other things being equal, these are actions that are right.

FORMALISM AND RULE UTILITARIANISM

Increasingly, contemporary attempts in ethics to formulate plausible utilitarian theories agree with Ross that many of our moral decisons are judged to be right or wrong because they do or do not conform with what we recognize to be moral principles or rules. Consequently, present utilitarians try to state utilitarianism in such a way that the rightness of acting in accord with moral principles will be somehow accounted for. In the light of this development, a distinction has been made between act utilitarianism and rule utilitarianism. There are those in moral philosophy who would argue that our discussion so far of the limitations of utilitarianism has been restricted to looking at the implications of act utilitarianism and has not yet addressed the advances in thinking formulated by rule utilitarians.

In his introduction to ethics, Paul Taylor has provided us with a very succinct statement of the distinction between act and rule utilitarianism.

> For all utilitarians, the principle of utility is the *ultimate* test of the rightness or wrongness of human conduct. But in applying this test, do we apply it directly to particular acts, or do we restrict its application to rules of conduct, and let those rules determine whether a particular act is right or wrong? In the first case, which is unrestricted or act-utilitarianism, we must find out what are the consequences of a *particular act* in order to know whether it is right or wrong. . . .
>
> According to restricted or rule-utilitarianism, on the other hand, an act is right if it conforms to a valid rule of conduct and wrong if it violates such a rule. And it is the test of utility that determines the validity of rules of conduct. Thus the one true normative ethical system binding upon all mankind is a set of rules such that, if people regulated their conduct by these rules, greater intrinsic value and less intrinsic disvalue would result for everyone than if they followed a different code.[14]

For purposes of this discussion, we will assume that Taylor's ambiguous reference to "people" is intended to mean either all people or some substantial amount of people sufficient to achieve the "greater intrinsic value" (a greater degree of happiness or pleasure) through regulating their conduct by a particular set of rules.

One might argue that rule utilitarianism conceived in this way allows us to recognize and guide our behavior in accord with moral principles of the sort enunciated by Ross, so that his objections to utilitarianism no longer apply. But why, then, be a rule utilitarian? Well, simply because a rule utilitarian does not rest the case for moral rules, as does Ross, upon an assumption that these are self-evident to reason; rather, it is argued, these rules are only justified by the ends they realize. Rule utilitarianism, therefore, would seem to overcome the apparent arbitrariness of claiming that we recognize and follow moral principles because reason tells us to do so, by providing an account of why it is reasonable to do so. According to Taylor, we can justify those moral principles which, "when generally complied with, bring about more happiness or pleasure for everyone and less unhappiness or pain than would result from general compliance with any other set of rules." [15]

At first glance it would appear that rule utilitarians have managed to retain all the advantages of Ross's work and have given us a bonus. Is this really the case, however? As we shall argue later, in chapter 7, we will not rest content, as did Ross, with considering moral principles to be grounded on self-evident intuitions known to reason. We would agree with rule utilitarians that there is a certain arbitrariness about this when clearly, over the centuries, there have been some disagreements as to what constitutes a rationally defensible set of moral principles. But the irony about the particular claim of the rule utilitarians is that while they reject any given set of moral rules as being rationally self-evident, they are asserting that at least one rule is always rational and apparently self-evidently so, because at least in some accounts, as in Taylor's, no defense of the rationality of utility is really offered. Indeed, as we shall see, the defense of utility is its presumed rationality.

It is interesting that Taylor sees no need for a defense of his view that a particular right-making characteristic, the one that utilitarians consider to be the ultimate test of rightness and wrongness, provides the reasons we accept and follow moral rules. Why is this? This is true because, as Taylor would have it:

> How else can we justify rules of conduct other than by showing the *purpose* for which rational beings would use them as guides to their conduct? Furthermore, if this purpose were anything other than the promotion of their happiness, could we consider such beings rational? The principle of utility, in short, is built into the very conception of a rational ground for rules of conduct.[16]

One way of interpreting what Taylor is saying here is that it is rational to recognize one of Ross's prima facie duties as self-evidently rational, namely, the duty to promote happiness. But is not that the very quarrel that we have between formalism and utilitarianism? It seems to many of us to be utterly rational to pursue justice, for example, as an end, as something intrinsically valuable. At this point, Taylor seems to be begging the question as to what moral principles are to be recognized as rational.

Taylor might reply that we are misunderstanding him. He might say, of course, we act exactly as if justice is an intrinsic value and that it is worth pursuing as an end in itself. But, he could say to us, would any of us pursue justice as an end if in doing so we promoted unhappiness, or at least more unhappiness than happiness? It may be true, he might concede, that in a given case people might sacrifice their own happiness for the sake of realizing justice, but surely in justifying their pursuit of justice they would not wish to create more unhappiness than already exists. Well, is that strictly true?

If the great majority of people in the world or in a given society were committed to a policy of genocide, such as the Nazi policy regarding Jews, for example, would we feel that it was wrong to make that genocidal majority unhappy by curbing their unjust policy of genocide? Assuming now that 60 percent of the world's population or of a given society's population favored genocide and assuming also that giving up this policy would make them unhappy, I, for one, would be quite willing to struggle for a world or a society in which this would happen. Leaving aside questions of how one would accomplish this in morally justifiable ways, the fact of their unhappiness at giving up genocide would not make it morally wrong to seek to put an end to genocidal policies perpetrated by a majority within a nation or among nations.

However, this brings us back to the very assumption of rule utilitarianism, namely, that everyone's happiness will be served by having people guided by moral rules such as justice. At the very least, rule utilitarians require some justification for the assumption that doing one's duty increases happiness even in the long run, and no one can offer us conclusive evidence for this. However, it is plausible to assume that if we consider justice, truth-telling, and the other prima facie duties enunciated by Ross as intrinsically valuable, that is, as worthy ends to pursue along with happiness, then it would make sense to assume that people will be happy in pursuing the ends that they value. In short, the plausibility of saying that happiness will follow from being just, honest, grateful, and so on, is that we do consider it reasonable and correct to guide our actions by such moral principles, and doing something that we consider to be right and correct is at the very least not something that pains and disturbs us and may understandably be accompanied by happiness. Indeed, Ross has argued, and in this context Taylor has not specifically addressed this argument, that knowledge and virtue are intrinsic goods that we pursue in addition to happiness or pleasure. At the very least, a rule utilitarian will have to confront such candidates for intrinsic value beyond happiness or pleasure.

Formalism does not deny that one of our obligations has to do with refraining from inflicting injury or pain on the one hand, and seeking to benefit others by increasing their pleasure on the other. The difference between the formalist and the rule utilitarian at this point is that neither of these moral obligations nor their combination in a principle of utility is seen as the only moral obligation and the only reasonable end to pursue. Ross's whole list of moral obligations is seen by the formalist as a set of reasonable ends to pursue.

There are, of course, real difficulties with the whole notion of happiness or pleasure. Indeed, as we shall argue in chapter 5, some definite limits should be put upon the extent to which we seek happiness or pleasure for ourselves and others. As we have already argued, we would surely have no moral obligation to increase the pleasure of those who achieve pleasure from genocidal acts. Indeed, we could very well posit an obligation to decrease such pleasure.

There is another point that needs to be raised in connection with the assumption that the best balance of happiness will follow if people use a certain set of moral rules as guidelines. There is really no way of testing this unless people were willing to try out a whole series of different sets over a sufficiently long period of time to be able to gather the data needed. One of the problems of the principle of utility, not only for rule utilitarians but for act utilitarians, is that we cannot really know what the consequences of our actions or of our rule-keeping will be. Indeed, it is very interesting in this respect that Taylor takes the view that act utilitarians will want to use moral rules as practical guides because there are some situations in which, as he says, "it is difficult or impossible to predict the consequences of alternative ways of acting." [17] This same assertion can be made about the difficulty or impossibility of predicting the consequences of following a particular set of rules rather than their alternatives. In short, we shall have to take up the whole question of why it is reasonable to recognize and follow certain moral principles, and we leave that for chapters 6, 7, and 8.

Taylor and others might say that we are failing to recognize something very important in all this, namely, that our social existence would be impossible if we did not develop and adhere to certain moral rules. This is a very important observation and one with which we have no quarrel. It is precisely what we have argued in the beginning of this chapter in defining the nature of moral principles; and this same line of reasoning will be developed even further in chapter 5. Our quarrel with rule utilitarianism is that the rationality of these very basic moral rules does not hinge solely on their necessity for community and their social function. And, certainly, the rationality of these basic rules or moral principles does not depend solely on whether they do or do not promote happiness, even though we may expect that they will.

There is one further difficulty with rule utilitarianism that merits at least brief comment. It is difficult to maintain the distinction between act and rule utilitarianism when, as Taylor asserts, "the principle of utility is the *ultimate* test of the rightness or wrongness of human conduct." [18] Note also that utility is something that is to be maximized, and disutility something to be minimized. Now when utility is seen as the ultimate test and as something to maximize, then it seems to me that it becomes the only moral principle. To argue that rule utilitarians accept several moral principles is in the end to argue that rule utilitarians are not morally conscientious. A morally conscientious rule utilitarian, like a morally conscientious act utilitarian, should never accept a given act as right if in following the moral rule that specifies its rightness, as for example an instance of truth-telling, to tell the truth would clearly make for more rather than less unhappiness. Of course, the rule utilitarian would retort, I should tell the truth even so, because it is best on the whole to put up with this particular increase of unhappiness for the sake of the greater happiness of people generally being truthful. But that brings us full circle around to how we know this to be true. If we know that someone will be killed because we tell the truth, we might very well want to make an exception to following the rule of truth-telling, and if we argue that killing creates much more unhappiness than lying, there is no difference between this argument and that of an act utilitarian. If a rule utilitarian wishes to argue that some moral rules are more weighty than others because of their greater utility, then once more utility becomes the determinative moral rule and functionally the only moral consideration in deciding the rightness or wrongness of our particular actions. It would take us too far afield to continue this debate. There are certainly those who have argued that there is no difference logically and practically between act and rule utilitarianism, and readers may pursue these issues further and judge this for themselves.[19]

In conclusion, we see no compelling reason for abandoning formalism for act or rule utilitarianism. Formalism as we have described and understood it in this chapter includes the concern of all utilitarians to weigh consequences in decisions about the rightness or wrongness of actions. But to restrict the weighing of consequences to considerations of something called utility or happiness or pleasure seems to us, as Ross contended, to oversimplify the kinds of things that are morally significant and are to be considered moral principles by which we guide our behavior.

In arguing the case for formalism and for a plural set of moral principles, we have relied exclusively on the work of W. D. Ross. We have not, however, intended to endorse in every respect Ross's particular way of characterizing each of the moral principles that he has identified. There are at least three moral concepts—beneficence, justice, and love of neighbor—that require further elaboration, in some instances to supplement and in some instances to correct his formulation of them. Thus, in chapters 4 and 5 we will examine the principle of beneficence and its relationship to what Ross calls the principle of "not injuring others" ("non-maleficence"). In chapter 5 we will also touch on the notions of justice and love of neighbor. The concept of love of neighbor has a long history of development within both philosophical and religious ethics, and Ross's failure to deal with it explicitly does, as we shall try to indicate, leave out some important considerations for moral conduct and ethical theory.

Chapter III—Suggestions for Further Reading

Brandt, Richard B. *Ethical Theory*. Englewood Cliffs, N.J.: Prentice-Hall, 1959.
   A systematic account from a utilitarian perspective.
Carritt, E. F. *The Theory of Morals: An Introduction to Ethical Philosophy*. London: Oxford University Press, 1928.
   An introduction to moral philosophy written explicitly from a formalist perspective. Written concisely and clearly.
Rawls, John. *A Theory of Justice*. Cambridge, Mass.: The Belknap Press of Harvard University Press, 1971.
   The most thorough and systematic contemporary formalist theory of justice.
Smart, J. J. C., and Williams, Bernard. *Utilitarianism: For and Against*. New York: Cambridge University Press, 1973.

chapter iv
conflicting views
of beneficence
in the euthanasia debate

Among the moral principles recognized and delineated by W. D. Ross is the principle of beneficence. As Ross depicted it, the principle of beneficence rests "on the mere fact that there are other beings in the world whose condition we can make better in respect of virtue, or of intelligence, or of pleasure." Beneficence, then, for Ross, means doing good. Virtue, intelligence, and pleasure are three states of mind that Ross recognizes as goods.[1]

Ross does not include the moral principle of not injuring others under the principle of beneficence. Rather, he argues that this principle of nonmaleficence is apprehended as distinct from that of beneficence. Furthermore, the obligation not to injure others is recognized to be of a more stringent character.

William K. Frankena agrees with Ross that doing good and not injuring others are distinguishable moral obligations. He agrees also with Ross that the duty not to injure others is more stringent than the duty to do good. It is true that Frankena considers the obligation not to injure others as an aspect of the moral principle of beneficence, not as a separate principle of nonmaleficence. But this difference between Frankena and Ross is not what concerns us here. Frankena has made some further distinctions in his articulation of the principle of beneficence that add a dimension not explicitly included in Ross, either under his understanding of beneficence or of maleficence. As this chapter will attempt to illustrate, these further refinements by Frankena are of considerable practical and theoretical import.

According to Frankena, the principle of beneficence says at least the following four things:

1. One ought not to inflict evil or harm (what is bad).
2. One ought to prevent evil or harm.
3. One ought to remove evil.
4. One ought to do or promote good.

Frankena goes on to argue that

these four things are different, but they may appropriately be regarded as parts of the principle of beneficence. Of the four, it is most plausible to say that (4) is not a duty in the strict sense. In fact, one is inclined to say that in some sense (1) takes precedence over (2), (2) over (3), and (3) over (4), other things being equal. But all are, at any rate, principles of prima facie duty.[2]

In the light of these distinctions, it is not clear what kind of priorities Ross would set with respect to preventing harm or injury and removing harm or injury. The question regarding priorities is an important one, particularly for medicine. It is no accident that after centuries of action and reflection, medicine honors the maxim "first of all, do no harm," giving not harming the same priority found in Frankena and Ross. Yet at the same time, medicine is often engaged in practices in which the prevention, and even more often the removal, of harm is considered more stringent an obligation than the obligation to refrain from injury. Various kinds of preventive and directly life-saving surgery provide actual instances of inflicting injury for the sake of preventing or removing some condition that will prove injurious or even fatal if nothing is done. The just-war criteria in ethics also recognize that those who fight in self-defense may have to inflict injury, even death, in order to prevent injury or death and in order to remove or stop aggressive actions that threaten to injure or kill others.[3] From a moral point of view, then, self-defense is another instance where the prevention of injury is regarded as a more stringent obligation than the obligation not to inflict injury.

One of the very critical contemporary debates regarding medical policy illustrates very well how difficult it is to decide when the most stringent duty not to inflict injury or death should or should not be set aside in favor of the prevention or removal of some kind of evil. I am thinking here of the debate regarding euthanasia. Within this debate regarding what it is that the principle of beneficence demands of us, the question as to what counts as evil arises with considerable urgency.

Increasingly, the word *euthanasia* is being used as a synonym for *mercy killing*. Originally the Greek word *euthanasia* meant "painless, happy death." This meaning still appears as one definition of the term. However, a second meaning is added that specifies that euthanasia is an "act or method of causing death painlessly, so as to end suffering: advocated by some as a way to deal with persons dying of incurable, painful diseases."[4] In the light of current usage and for purposes of this discussion, I am using *mercy killing* and *euthanasia* as synonyms for "the deliberate inducement of a quick, painless death."

Some have claimed that under certain circumstances, euthanasia is beneficent and that therefore euthanasia is sometimes morally obligatory. This is a claim that deserves careful scrutiny if we are to strive for moral conscientiousness. What follows now is a discussion of one particular set of arguments for and against euthanasia as a form of beneficence. It should not be considered a complete and definitive discussion of euthanasia as such, but it does indicate some of the very strong reasons people have for both accepting and rejecting euthanasia as a practice, and it also presents an alternative to euthanasia, the basis for which is a different conception of what beneficence requires of us as morally conscientious persons.

THE ETHIC OF BENEFICENT EUTHANASIA

One of the most compelling cases for beneficent euthanasia has been offered by the philosopher Marvin Kohl.[5] According to Kohl, all of us have a prima facie obligation to act kindly. For the purposes of indicating when euthanasia would be an act of kindness, he specifies the following sense in which an act can be described as kind.

> An act is kind if it (a) is intended to be helpful; (b) is done so that, if there be any expectation of receiving remuneration (or the like), the individual would nonetheless act even if it became apparent that there was little chance of his expectation being realized; and (c) results in beneficial treatment for the intended recipient. The Boy or Girl Scout helping an elderly man or woman cross the street, or the proverbial Good Samaritan, are paradigm cases of kindness.

From this definition of kindness, Kohl argues that

> the necessary, and perhaps sufficient, conditions for beneficent euthanasia are that the act must involve a painless inducement to a quick death; that the act must result in beneficial treatment for the intended recipient; and that, aside from the desire to help the recipient, no other considerations are relevant [a combination of conditions (a) and (b)].[6]

To clarify further what he means by "beneficent euthanasia," Kohl offers the reader two paradigm cases. The first case involves: (1) patients suffering from an irremediable condition like cancer (carcinomatosis); (2) patients with severe pain; (3) patients clearly dying as a result of their condition; (4) patients voluntarily in favor of some means of "easy death"; and (5) the fact that apart from the desire to help such patients, no other circumstances are relevant. Kohl cites another type of case as a paradigm: a child (1) born without limbs, sight, hearing, or a functioning cerebral cortex; (2) suffering no pain; (3) for whom death is not imminent; and (4) aside from the desire to help the patient, no other conditions are relevant. These two types of cases are quite different in Kohl's mind except in two important respects: both involve serious and irremediable physical conditions and arouse in others a wish to help. Kohl argues that in both types of circumstances, induced death would probably be considered an act of kindness by most persons. Kohl underlines the importance of this claim because "if true it means that considerations of free choice, the imminence of death, and/or the existence of pain are not always relevant, at least not to judgments of kindness." [7]

With these paradigms in mind and on the assumption that societies and their individual members have a prima facie obligation to treat one another kindly, Kohl infers quite logically that beneficent euthanasia, because it is a species of kindness, is a prima facie obligation. This conclusion seems obvious to Kohl, but he realizes that it is not obvious to everyone, given certain objections that have been raised against euthanasia. Kohl, therefore, feels constrained to take up three such objections and offer what he takes to be refutations of them:

1) Against "edge of the wedge" claims, he argues that a policy of beneficent euthanasia will result in minimizing suffering and maximizing kindly treatment.

2) Against claims that homicide is intrinsically unjust, he argues that beneficent euthanasia satisfies a fundamental need for human dignity.

3) Against those who claim that we are not obligated to kill, even out of kindness, he argues that failure to give help in the form of beneficent euthanasia is a failure to live up to the Good Samaritan ideal.

1) *The "Wedge" Argument.* Kohl interprets the "wedge" by claiming that if beneficent euthanasia is morally justified, then

euthanasia that cannot be considered beneficent will come to be practiced and justified. He sees "wedge" arguments as being based upon two assumptions: first, all theories of euthanasia ultimately rest upon a principle of utility; and second, all theories of utility resemble those held by the Nazis, the implication being that great cruelty rather than kindness will result.

Kohl disassociates himself from any view that would advocate euthanasia for economic purposes. He distinguishes this kind of utility from beneficence. The duty of beneficence is in his view the duty to minimize suffering and to maximize kindly treatment. If there is a "slippery slide" that results from policies of beneficent euthanasia, it will be in the direction of minimizing suffering and maximizing kindly treatment. Second, he distinguishes between the kindest way of doing a particular act X, such as killing, and the kindest way of treating a human being as a human being, which may not include doing X or killing at all. Beneficent euthanasia has for its objective not only death with dignity but living and dying with dignity. Killing is only kind under very limited circumstances, and not under the numerous circumstances that led to Nazi atrocities. Again, the goal is to minimize suffering and to maximize kindness, and to do this for everyone.

In dealing with the "wedge" argument, however, Kohl has not yet confronted it in its most powerful form. A "wedge" argument does not have to predict that certain practices will follow from another. Its primary concern is with the form or logic of moral justifications.

Consider, for example, Kohl's point that it is morally obligatory to practice beneficent euthanasia sometimes when the person killed does not choose death, is not dying, and is not in pain. It is very difficult to see why this would not justify involuntary euthanasia. Suppose, however, that Kohl is not bothered by this, and, indeed, he is not. The next question that arises is that of procuring agreement as to the narrowness or broadness of the categories of persons to be appropriate candidates for mercy killing. Presumably the criterion that would for Kohl keep the category of cases narrowly defined is that of preserving the dignity of human beings. A child born without limbs, sight, hearing, or a functioning cerebral cortex, although not in pain and not dying, is for Kohl lacking in dignity, or in any event, will be treated with dignity by being painlessly put to death.

But what the "wedge" argument is saying is that there is no logical or easily agreed upon reason why the range of cases should be restricted to Kohl's paradigms or why it would not be beneficial to extend the range even beyond the retarded. For example, some people have argued that those with Down's syndrome, however happy and however in some instances educable, are also lacking in dignity so that their lives need not always be sustained even when they could be. Or there are instances where quadriplegics, who are fully conscious and rational, are not asked whether they wish to live or die but are drugged and deprived of life support so that they die.[8] The justification for this is logically the same as the justification for beneficent euthanasia in the case of the severely retarded. The physician considers the life of a quadriplegic or of someone with Down's syndrome to be undignified, or filled with suffering, or for other reasons not worth living. Such physicians certainly see themselves acting out of kindness.

The point of the "wedge" argument is very simple. Killing is generally wrong and should be kept to as narrow a range of exceptions as possible. The argument for beneficent euthanasia, unlike arguments for killing in self-defense, can apply logically to either a narrow or a wide range of cases; and the reasons for keeping the range of cases narrow are not reasons on which people will easily agree. Whether beneficent euthanasia will be applied to a narrow range of cases does not depend simply on how kind a society is. It will depend also on the various notions that are held as to what constitutes a dignified or meaningful human life. About this there have always been and will likely continue to be widespread differences of opinion, many of them based on implicit or explicit theological assumptions.

The "wedge" argument also warns against adopting the principle of minimizing suffering and maximizing kindness. It sounds right, but its logical implications go far beyond that which is intended by Kohl. If minimizing suffering is accomplished by killing, then it is logical to infer that killing, since it is a quicker, more painless way to alleviate suffering, is morally preferable to the provision of companionship and care for those who are either dying or recuperating from long-term illnesses, because such care is neither quick nor painless. Kohl would reject this interpretation of what is implied when he advocates minimizing suffering and maximizing kindness. Clearly, Kohl does not want to minimize suffering by resort to killing, but only by resort to killing out of kindness. Only those acts of killing that are at the same time acts of kindness are morally right and obligatory. On Kohl's view, then, we are obligated to be beneficent, and acts of kindness are definite instances of beneficence.

The question remains, however, as to what is to be considered kind or beneficent. Kohl has suggested two paradigmatic sets of circumstances in which killing is to be considered beneficent or kind. Kohl, like Frankena and Ross, undoubtedly wishes to continue to recognize the general stringency of the prohibition against killing but at the same time wishes to recognize certain limited circumstances under which the moral obligation to remove and prevent injury or harm—in this instance, suffering—takes precedence over the prohibition against killing. We shall come later to the point in Kohl's position when he specifically clarifies the sense in which kindness is to include the obligations to remove and prevent harm in the form of suffering, though this means inflicting injury in the form of death.

2) *Euthanasia as Unjust.* Kohl argues that beneficent euthanasia is consistent with justice because it meets a basic need for dignity and self-respect. Such dignity is clearly expressed when people ask for a quick and painless death when they see only pain and suffering as their lot. But Kohl does not want to restrict euthanasia to instances where consent can be obtained. Sometimes, he contends, neither justice nor dignity is served when the misery of an individual increases and consent is not possible.

Here again we see that there are instances in which Kohl would claim the inducement of a painless, quick death puts an end to a life of indignity. As we noted previously, it is difficult to know how wide a range of cases should be included among those where relief from indignity requires morally a nonvoluntarily induced, painless death. Those who induce this death will no doubt have varying notions as to what kind of misery and how much of it renders a life undignified. This is precisely what the "wedge" argument is concerned with. If euthanasia is practiced on others by someone like Kohl, it will be used as a last resort. If, however, there is a general policy of considering beneficent euthanasia a moral obligation and hence also existing laws that permit people to live up to their obligations, the practices may be quite different from those that Kohl would envisage and sanction. This would not be true because killing is contagious (Kohl has quite properly objected to that argument) but because the notion of dignity is open to a very wide range of meanings and agreement hard to obtain. This means that people would also not agree as to when it is kind to kill someone. It begs the question to tell us, as Kohl does, that most of us would consider it kind to kill in the two types of cases he takes to be paradigmatic. The question remains as to whether killing *ought to be* viewed as kind in such instances. Should we accept the view that, under the special circumstances cited by Kohl, the obligation to remove and prevent further harm in the form of suffering is more stringent than the obligation not to harm in the form of killing?

3) *The Obligation to Avoid Killing*. Kohl recognizes that there are some who will argue that one is not obligated to help the suffering in every way possible, particularly if such help entails killing. On Kohl's view, an important assumption in that argument is that cruelty is to be avoided. But, he contends, beneficent euthanasia also seeks to avoid cruelty. The difference between opponents and proponents of euthanasia here is over the meaning of what constitutes cruelty and whether avoidance of cruelty is morally sufficient. Kohl argues that those who oppose euthanasia on grounds that it is cruel interpret cruelty in a narrow sense to mean deliberately causing unnecessary pain or harm. They do not use the broader sense of the term *cruelty* that refers both to deliberately causing pain and to allowing needless pain or harm.[9] Allowing harm is, for Kohl, equivalent to failing to take positive steps to remove and prevent harm. Opponents of euthanasia, Kohl contends, are too prone to tolerate human misery of the sort illustrated by his paradigmatic cases.

Kohl calls this desire to avoid cruelty in the form of inflicting harm a "taboo" morality. It tells us what not to do, but not what to do. A society that avoids inflicting harm is admittedly better than one that does not. However, this "taboo" morality is, he contends, contrary to the ideal of the Good Samaritan who, unlike those who walk past the injured or the sick, seeks to help. Aversion to cruelty in the sense of not inflicting harm on anyone is not a sufficient principle of action if it does not also include the obligation to help and be beneficent to others by removing and preventing the evil of suffering. Kohl's notion of beneficence, then, like Frankena's, includes obligations to remove and prevent harm. His accusation against opponents of euthanasia is that they fail to satisfy the principle of beneficence in all its aspects. Concretely, what this means, according to Kohl, is that opponents of euthanasia will not, under the circumstances he specifies, take positive steps to do good and to prevent and remove harm in the form of suffering.

These arguments by Kohl are rather uncharacteristic of his usual fairness to opponents. Those who oppose euthanasia because it is an act of killing share with the Good Samaritan the concern to do good and to alleviate suffering by caring for somebody who is or may be dying. That is surely one of the major reasons for opposing euthanasia—namely, to care for people who are still alive and to help them make the most of life, relieving pain and suffering as much as is possible without purposely killing them. Kohl is assuming that the Good Samaritan ideal of practicing beneficence views the priorities regarding what is beneficent exactly the way he does in advocating beneficent euthanasia. On Kohl's view, if the dying man on the road to Jericho had asked the Good Samaritan to help him by making his death painless and quick, the Good Samaritan would have been obligated to do so, depending upon whether he felt that the injured man was indeed painfully and imminently dying. But is it self-evident that being a Good Samaritan would entail this obligation?

We see then how we have come about full circle. In effect, Kohl is taking the position that only proponents of euthanasia wish positively to do good and to prevent and remove suffering, and that opponents of euthanasia are simply trying to avoid inflicting harm in the form of killing and are so bent on it that they are not willing or able to be beneficent in the other senses in which he is using this term. Whether or not one favors euthanasia and whether or not it is considered a moral obligation would seem, then, to depend on one's notion of what is beneficent. The very understanding of a powerful paradigm of beneficence—the Good Samaritan ideal—is in dispute. Does the Good Samaritan ideal make a moral obligation out of mercy killing as Kohl argues? Is it possible to be committed to the Good Samaritan ideal of beneficence as a moral obligation but reject euthanasia as beneficent?

THE GOOD SAMARITAN IDEAL: AN ETHIC OF "BENEMORTASIA"

Because euthanasia no longer functions as a merely descriptive term for a happy or good death, it is necessary to invent some term for this purpose. I have chosen the word *benemortasia* which is derived from two familiar Latin words, *bene* (good) and *mors* (death). What *bene* in benemortasia means depends upon the ethical framework that one adopts in order to interpret what it is to experience a good death or at least what would be the most morally responsible way to behave in the face of death, either one's own or that of another. The ethic of benemortasia being suggested in what follows is one such ethical framework viewing beneficence and kindness in ways that provide policy alternatives to beneficent euthanasia.

The ethical framework for benemortasia I wish the reader to reflect upon recognizes beneficence as a moral principle. Beneficence includes at least three kinds of moral obligations: the obligation to prevent harm or maleficence, the obligation to remove what is harmful or maleficent, and the obligation to do what is good or morality supporting. In addition to and distinct from the principle of beneficence is the principle of nonmaleficence, the obligation not to harm others. The principle of nonmaleficence is generally, other things being equal, a more stringent obligation than beneficence.

Kohl does not include the obligation not to harm or injure in his definition of kindness. In short, he links kindness with beneficence, but not with nonmaleficence. Yet he does recognize the moral obligation not to harm or injure others. But in favoring euthanasia, he has taken the position that under certain specified circumstances, killing can be interpreted as an act of kindness, i.e., that it is sometimes more merciful to kill than to refrain from killing. Kohl further believes that the story of the Good Samaritan lends support to his view.

Let us look first, then, at the story of the Good Samaritan. Contrary to Kohl's interpretation, it would seem to me that the Good Samaritan ideal, when properly understood, includes in its notion of kindness the principle of nonmaleficence as well as that of beneficence. Recognition of the obligation not to kill is very much a part of the overall context in which the story of the Good Samaritan is told.

The injunction not to kill is part of a total effort to prevent the destruction of human beings and human communities. It is a universal prohibition in the sense that no society can be indifferent about the taking of human life. Any act insofar as it is an act of taking a human life is wrong, that is to say, taking a human life is a wrong-making characteristic of actions.[10] The obligation not to kill is the most stringently obligatory form of the principle of nonmaleficence.

Within the history of the West, the necessity for a prohibition against killing was recognized under intensely dramatic circumstances. A band of slaves found themselves in the midst of a desert, having escaped from oppression. They had to pull together or perish together under the harshest of conditions. As the very basis of their community, these slaves, now free, chose to unite themselves around certain definite constraints, including the pledge not to kill one another. Liberated from their bondage, they now pledged themselves not to injure one another in the form of stealing, bearing false witness, infidelity, and killing. This newly formed community was bound together by what has come to be known as the Mosaic covenant (the Ten Commandments—Ex. 20:1-17; Deut. 5:6-21).[11]

In the story of the Good Samaritan, a lawyer allegedly confronted Jesus with the question, "What shall I do to inherit eternal life?" (Luke 10:25). In other words, what must I do if I am to attain a complete life, one in which I realize myself to the utmost? Jesus inquired whether he knew the law, and the lawyer said he did. To show that he did, the lawyer responded with a rabbinic summary of the law well known to Jesus at that time: "You shall love the Lord your God with all your heart, and with all your soul, and with all your strength, and with all your mind; and your neighbor as yourself"(Luke 10:27). The lawyer did not recite the whole Mosaic covenant, but there is no question that the summary he gave included, and was meant to include, the obligation not to kill one's neighbors.

What is often forgotten about the story of the Good Samaritan is that Jesus was reportedly completely satisfied with this reply by the lawyer. He told the lawyer that he had given the right answer and that if he did what this rabbinic summary called for, he would live. Within the context, then, of this incident, Jesus in no way questioned the constraint against killing and the applicability of this constraint as a form of kindness to one's neighbor.

But the lawyer seems to have been a very contemporary figure because he asked the questions that keep getting asked over and over again today: Who is my neighbor? Who are the ones that I am to love by restraining myself against acts of killing, stealing, and the like?

It is at this point that Jesus introduced the well-known story about the Samaritan who, while on the road to Jericho, unlike others who passed by, stopped to aid a person who was half dead, who had been robbed, beaten, and left to die. There is also no suggestion in this story that one should think in the least about whether the dying person qualified for care. Indeed, after telling the story, Jesus asked the lawyer to tell him who was the neighbor to the one who was in need. The lawyer grasped the point of the story and said it was the Samaritan as contrasted with those who had walked by without caring at all for the wounded person. In short, neighbors are people who care.

We see, then, that the Good Samaritan ideal understands kindness as a pledge to be the type of person who provides care for those who need it. There is nothing in the story that suggests that someone is beyond our care or that someone in need does not qualify for it. And certainly there is nothing in the story that suggests that killing is a form of mercy or kindness. Indeed, the context within which the story is told links loving one's neighbor with the obligations cited in the Mosaic covenant, which include a general prohibition against killing.

Advocates of beneficent euthanasia would generally agree that one should not kill innocent people, particularly those who are as powerless to defend themselves as the dying and the handicapped, and also that people in need should receive care. They are skeptical, however, about the kind of care that can and will be provided to relieve pain and suffering by those who reject mercy killing.

As I see it, an ethic of benemortasia can offer at least the following kinds of care to patients who are considered to be imminently dying: (1) relief of pain; (2) relief of suffering; (3) respect for patients' rights to refuse treatment; and (4) administering of health care regardless of ability to pay. These four care provisions are in accord with the desire to be as beneficent as possible without, as Kohl would have us do, deliberately violating the principle of nonmaleficence. The concern is less with removing harm than with mitigating and preventing harm, the sources of which are pain, suffering, poverty, and loss of one's basic right to make moral choices.

1) *Relief of Pain*. There is widespread agreement among those who oppose beneficent euthanasia but who believe in mercy that pain relief should be made available to patients even when it means shortening the dying process. This is not considered killing or assisting in a killing, because the cause of death is the patient's terminal illness, and the shortening of the dying process has to do with a choice on the part of patients to live with less pain during their last days. All of us make choices about whether or not we will seek pain relief. While we are not terminally ill, we also make choices about the kind of care we will or will not seek. There is no reason to deny such freedom to someone who is dying. Indeed, there is every reason to be especially solicitous of a person whose days are known to be numbered. There is no legal or moral objection to the administration of pain relief provided it is for that purpose and not for the purpose of killing someone. This means that one does not knowingly give an overdose of pain relief, but rather concentrates on dosages that are sufficient for relief of pain even though at some point the final dose may well be administered.[12]

2) *Relief of Suffering*. Suffering is not the same as pain, although in instances where pain is extremely excruciating, it is virtually impossible to avoid suffering. We know, for example, that physicians can relieve suffering in a variety of ways. There is some evidence that patients who know they are dying generally suffer less and are less inclined to ask for pain relief than those who do not know that they are dying. We know also that one of the major sources of suffering of dying people can come from loneliness and lack of companionship. Our ethic of benemortasia would consider it not only kind but part of good care in the strictest medical sense to make provision for companionship, whether with medical, paramedical, or other persons brought to the hospital expressly for this purpose. Religious and other voluntary organizations often assist in these ways.[13]

3) *Patients' Rights to Refuse Treatment.* Dying patients are also living patients. They retain the same rights as everyone else voluntarily to leave the hospital or to refuse specific kinds of care. Indeed, this right is legally recognized. No new law is required to allow patients to exercise their rights. One of the important effects of the whole discussion of euthanasia is that all of us, including health professionals, are becoming more sensitive to this right to refuse care. At the same time, however, given the concern to save lives and to refrain from killing, one would continue to expect that physicians, in instances when they see some hope of saving lives, would usually presuppose the consent of their patients to strive for their lives even when such patients may be expressing a wish to die. Many desperately sick people have despaired of life temporarily but are later grateful to be alive and well.

Those who are irreversibly comatose or those who, as in Kohl's paradigm, have no functioning of the cerebral cortex, no use of limbs, et cetera, pose special difficulties both for an ethic of beneficent euthanasia as well as an ethic of benemortasia. We are dealing in these cases with very tragic circumstances. No decision we make is totally satisfactory from a moral point of view. From the standpoint of our ethic of benemortasia, there is a strong presumption to continue to support the comatose and the severely brain damaged until there is no reasonable hope of improving or reversing their condition. And when such a point is reached despite every effort, it may be kind to withdraw from massive, sustained efforts—involving a respirator, for example—in the face of the next serious bout of illness where such episodes are expected to continue and be frequent until fatal. The difference between beneficent euthanasia and our ethic of benemortasia is that whereas the former would deliberately induce death, the latter as a last resort, after making every effort to save and repair life, mercifully retreats to "caring only" in the face of continuously devastating illness when these mark the prelude to death's inevitability. It would take us too far afield to discuss the various interpretations of what *"caring only"* means, and this has been done well elsewhere.[14]

4) *Universal Health Care.* In order to be kind as well as just in the provision of care for dying and severely brain-damaged people, no single person or family should have to bear alone the burden of extensive medical costs. It is notorious that poor people

are more often and much sooner let go as dying persons than those who have ample financial resources. Discussions of beneficent euthanasia should not overlook such injustices to people in need of care.

Proponents of beneficent euthanasia would accept the desirability of showing kindness in the ways we have indicated, but they would not agree that kindness can always be fully satisfied without *inducing* death. Under certain circumstances specified by Kohl, kindness demands a *quick, painless* death. An ethic of benemortasia, on the other hand, seeks to reduce pain and suffering as much as possible but not to the point of directly inducing death. This difference between the policy of beneficent euthanasia and the policy of benemortasia as here depicted revolves around differing notions of kindness and beneficence despite large areas of agreement as to what constitutes kindness.

Kohl, as an advocate of beneficent euthanasia, equates kindness with beneficence. Beneficence is considered to be a right-making characteristic of actions and policies. Kindness, therefore, is one of our moral obligations. According to Kohl, there are situations when failing to induce death is precisely to fail to be kind, and this is morally wrong.

Kohl's examples are designed to indicate the kind of situation in which he sees it morally wrong to fail to induce death. How can killing be a form of beneficence for Kohl? It can be when killing is an instance of preventing cruelty, that is, of minimizing suffering. The reader will recall that the failure to prevent or remove the evil of suffering is a failure to be kind. If, then, we are to maximize kindness, Kohl would argue that this would involve in his paradigmatic cases the direct inducement of death to minimize suffering.

On the face of it, it seems right to consider ourselves obligated to maximize kindness and to minimize suffering and to do those actions that accomplish both at the same time. However, what makes kindness morally right or wrong? It is not enough to say that being kind is being helpful, even though it would certainly be the case that being unhelpful would not be kind. Presumably what controls the meaning of kindness for Kohl in the case of euthanasia is the notion of dignity. Imminently dying cancer patients who are in great pain and wish to die will be treated with dignity if their request to be killed is honored and will lose dignity if it is not. The infant without a functioning cerebral cortex will lead an undignified life until it is killed. To wait until such a child dies is to tolerate the indignity of its living in a certain state of being. Because of the indignities of certain states of being and of failing to have certain requests honored, Kohl is assuming that we can only minimize suffering and maximize kindness by engaging in a direct act of killing.

It is interesting to note that Kohl is able to bypass a serious moral dilemma in his argument by excluding from his notion of beneficence the obligation not to harm or injure others. He clearly recognizes that cruelty includes inflicting harm as well as failing to prevent and remove what is harmful, so that in order to minimize suffering, cruelty must be avoided. Thus, one can presumably infer that to be kind means also to refrain from inflicting harm or injury. But insofar as others may argue that killing is the ultimate in cruelty, it is not clear from Kohl's writing whether killing has anything to do with cruelty at all. And since kindness is linked with a notion of beneficence that does not include a notion of maleficence, Kohl is able to argue in terms of maximizing beneficence without asking whether this also involves maximizing nonmaleficence. The restraint against killing is not specifically recognized either as part of Kohl's notion of kindness or as a separate principle of nonmaleficence. If it were, it would be much less clear that our moral obligation to be kind would also include a moral obligation, under certain circumstances, to induce death. To be sure, Kohl recognizes that killing in general is wrong. But in this particular instance, the moral obligation to be kind, in terms of beneficence, is more stringent than the moral obligation not to kill. In fact, according to Kohl, the moral obligation to be kind and to maximize kindness is in some instances precisely the moral obligation to inflict harm in the form of killing. Logically, this can only come about if the obligation to prevent and remove harm is considered more stringent than the obligation not to harm and not to kill. Because of his failure to give equal or greater priority to the notion or principle of nonmaleficence, Kohl's particular type of moral reasoning and his interpretation of what is kind run counter to the notion of kindness underlying the ethic of benemortasia as here presented. To be kind is to do what is beneficent as well as to refrain from what is maleficent, and that includes refraining from killing. If kindness is to be maximized at all, then on this view, unlike that of Kohl, both the obligation to be beneficent and the obligation to refrain from killing would have to be maximized. Simply maximizing kindness would not by itself establish any priority between the obligation to remove and prevent suffering on the one hand and the obligation to refrain from killing on the other.

With respect to establishing priorities, I think it is essential to recognize that any principle of maximization provides only an apparent solution which in the end is doomed to fail. Frankena quite properly identifies the view that we have an obligation to maximize, that is, an obligation to do those actions that will bring about the best balance of good over evil, as a principle of utility. He notes that if we grant such a principle of maximization higher priority than other principles, we would always have to prefer a net balance of one hundred units of good over evil where some evil is produced by our actions, practices, or rules, to those actions, practices, or rules that would produce ninety-nine units of good but no evil. Frankena does not want to equate the principle of beneficence with such a principle of utility because he would wish to leave open the possibility that we might prefer ninety-nine units of good from an action that produces no evil to an action that produces one hundred units of good but also results in some evil. [15] One reason for this is that we cannot actually always quantify good and evil, and so we are not always in a position to know how to count units of good and evil. How many units of good, for example, should outweigh the evil of killing someone? Or to return to Kohl's use of the maximization principle, i.e., maximizing kindness and minimizing suffering, how much suffering justifies its eradication by an act of killing? When is suffering more of an evil than being killed? How confident can we be about a judgment that, in certain instances, our obligation to stop someone from suffering is more stringent than our obligation not to kill them?

In our ethic of benemortasia, we have argued for upholding one of the traditional ethical priorities established in medicine—namely, that physicians and other health professionals see themselves as strictly obligated, first of all, to do no harm. Where it is decided that it is right to inflict injury on patients, it is on the grounds that life and health will be better served by causing such injury—for example, surgery—and that, if not in the short run certainly in the long run, pain and suffering will be diminished by such intervention. Health professionals are in the business of saving lives as well as caring for those whose lives they cannot save, and their interventions are first and foremost restrained by the desire and the obligation not to do anything harmful to any of their patients. If the risk of dying from intervention is less than the risk of failing to intervene, then other things being equal, physicians have a moral basis for weighing more heavily the obligation to prevent and/or remove some condition that is life threatening. Even so, this is done wherever possible with the explicit consent of the patient or the patient's relatives.

Our ethic of benemortasia does not say that one can never justify killing or subjecting someone to the risk of death. But if one is to justify killing, it will have to be for something that does not undermine the usual presumption that life is precious and that everyone has an equal right to life. This means that one can sometimes justify ending a life to save a life as, for example, in a case of trying to prevent a murder or in a case of abortion to save a woman's life. Such an act is not kind insofar as killing is involved; rather, it is kind because a life is saved. The killing is a tragic by-product of what it took in a given instance to protect and save life. In short, on this view kind actions are those that satisfy the principles of both beneficence and nonmaleficence so far as it is possible in situations of conflict.

Kohl, however, using the notion of dignity to decide when an act is kind, is convinced that kindness in the form of killing to prevent and remove suffering is right in special circumstances when human dignity is served. It is precisely this appeal to some notion of dignity to justify killing that evokes ''wedge'' arguments. As I indicated previously, there are serious and widespread differences among people as to what constitutes human dignity. If who will live and who will die is made contingent upon these widely divergent views of human dignity, moral and legal policies that justify mercy killing can in principle justify a very narrow or a very wide range of instances in which it will be claimed that we as a society are obligated to kill someone.

The debate concerning what constitutes human dignity is not one that can be easily resolved. There are deep philosophical and religious differences that divide people here. The injunction not to kill is not divisive in this way. A great deal of the emotion generated by the debate over euthanasia finds its source precisely in the understandable and deep uneasiness of a large number of individuals when they are asked to move away from a stringent obligation to refrain from acts of killing, regarding the stringency of which there is widespread agreement, and to make judgments about who shall live and who shall die on the basis of conceptions of human dignity characterized by profound religious, ethnic, philosophical, and other differences.

In view of the widespread tendency to equate kindness or mercy with beneficence and to make the meaning of kindness hinge on a very subjective notion like dignity, it is quite understandable why medical and other professional schools have been reluctant to think of love or kindness as something that can or should be taught. After all, what predictable content can be given to something like the Good Samaritan ideal? If, however, one conceptualizes the Good Samaritan ideal as we have, it is very much in line with the long-standing wisdom of the medical profession in acknowledging as a basic standard "first of all, do no harm." Since these principles can be rationally articulated and taught, it is possible to teach kindness as expressed in the Good Samaritan ideal. But kindness refers not only to moral principles that guide actions and practices but also to the will to do what is right and the ability to discern it. This aspect of kindness is described in chapter 5 briefly and then again in chapter 8. Kindness in this sense can also be taught.

In the present chapter, we have indicated how certain methods of moral reasoning dispose one toward accepting or rejecting euthanasia as a moral obligation. It remains to be seen in subsequent chapters what various grounds exist for accepting a general constraint against taking life and what differences in thinking dispose one to narrow or to broaden the range of exceptions to this general constraint.

Although Kohl has left himself open to a "wedge" argument, more is at stake in the difference between the moral thinking behind Kohl's case for beneficent euthanasia and our own framework for an ethic of benemortasia. We need to examine still further the concepts of kindness, of doing good, and of refraining from harming others. Therefore, we shall try to indicate in the next chapter some further reasons the obligation not to kill is so stringent and why kindness and doing good have to be understood in ways that do not undermine or destroy other moral principles.

Chapter IV—Suggestions for Further Reading

The following books provide introductions to medical ethics as well as specific chapters and sections on euthanasia as such. These books are representative of the thinking of contemporary moral philosophers, Jewish and Protestant ethicists, and Roman Catholic moral theologians.

Gorovitz, Samuel, et al., eds. *Moral Problems in Medicine*. Englewood Cliffs, N.J.: Prentice-Hall, 1976.

A set of readings on a number of topics in medical ethics.

Häring, Bernard. *Medical Ethics*. Notre Dame, Indiana: Fides Publishers, 1973.

Kelly, Gerald, S.J. *Medico-Moral Problems*. St. Louis, Mo.: Catholic Hospital Association, 1959.

Reiser, Stanley; Dyck, Arthur J.; and Curran, William, eds. *Ethics in Medicine*. Cambridge, Mass.: MIT Press, 1977.

An anthology of considerable scope covering many topics and containing essays by medical professionals, moral philosophers, lawyers, and religious ethicists.

Rosner, Fred. *Modern Medicine and Jewish Law: Studies in Torah Judaism*. New York: Bloch Publishing Co., 1972.

Smith, Harmon L. *Ethics and the New Medicine*. Nashville: Abingdon Press, 1970.

A somewhat different Protestant perspective from the one found in Paul Ramsey's *Patient as Person* cited in n. 14 this chapter.

chapter v
moral requisites of community: love of neighbor

In the previous chapter, we noted that the Good Samaritan story contains the notion of love, or love of neighbor. Upon analysis of that story, we concluded that love of neighbor, insofar as it is an expression of kindness, refers to acts in conformity with the principle of nonmaleficence as well as the principle of beneficence. In short, to love one's neighbor is to refrain from inflicting evil on the one hand, and to do good on the other.[1]

We also saw that though Kohl invokes the Good Samaritan as a paradigm of kindness, kindness on his view does not necessarily include adherence to a principle of nonmaleficence. In some instances, then, Kohl justifies euthanasia because the obligation to do good through removing and preventing suffering can be more stringent than the obligation to refrain from killing. The decision as to whether to agree or disagree with Kohl on this point will depend at least in part on one's specific understanding of what is evil. Are there grounds on which to consider some evils as having much more moral weight than others?

Loving one's neighbor within the context of the Good Samaritan story does offer a significant clue as to where to look in any investigation of what counts as evil. Loving one's neighbor within that context refers to a set of prohibitions against evil specified within what has come to be known as the Mosaic covenant (the Ten Commandments—Ex. 20:1-17; Deut. 5:6-21). It is interesting to note that the Mosaic covenant arose as a direct response to a problem that is not directly dealt with by the discussions of beneficence and nonmaleficence, as these are usually conducted within moral philosophy. The problem posed in this agreement of a band of liberated slaves traversing a barren, hostile desert environment is precisely one of trying to specify the most basic associations or institutions that are morally requisite to forming and sustaining a community. It was in addressing this kind of issue that it became necessary to formulate the most community-threatening forms of evil.

In addition to indicating what counts as evil and what counts as good, the story of the Good Samaritan raises another kind of issue for normative ethics, namely, what it means to be a good person. Being a Good Samaritan is not only to perform and to refrain from certain kinds of acts, but it is also to be a certain kind of person, one who is disposed toward showing love or kindness (in the form of doing good and refraining from evil).

In this chapter, then, we will examine love of neighbor in its three major aspects: (1) as a constraint upon inflicting harm or evil; (2) as a form of doing good; and (3) as a disposition or trait of persons.

CONSTRAINTS AGAINST EVIL AS MORAL REQUISITES OF COMMUNITY

We have already called attention to the dramatic circumstances under which the Mosaic covenant was said to be formulated. Though political in language and form, the Mosaic covenant is both a religious and a moral document.[2] Our interest in the covenant at this point is focused on the extent to which it specifies what it means to love one's neighbor. This it does by stating what are perceived to be moral constituents of community. If one is to have community at all, and if there is to be some kind of cooperative association among individual members of a group, all of whom have their peculiarities, needs, and aspirations, certain moral obligations to form community and to refrain from acts or policies that would be evil because they are destructive of human associations or institutions would need to be identified, acknowledged, and, for the most part, acted upon.

If a community is at all to extend into the future, it must have continuity with its past. Thus, some form of honor, gratitude, or recognition would have to be given to those who procreate and rear children. So it is not astonishing that the first kind of neighbor relation that is enjoined in the Mosaic covenant is that of "honoring" mothers and fathers. To that injunction the promise is added that if this is done, the future of one's parents and one's children will have in one sense been secured. Only if parents and being parents are positively valued, is there any possibility at all for the socialization of children and the continuation of a people.[3] Obviously if no one thought well of parents and no one wanted to be one, any group would die when those who act on that attitude die. This, then, can quite properly be seen as a primary moral requisite of any community if it is to have a future. It is also true that should procreation continue on the part of those who utterly repudiate their parents, the human species could continue, but not a particular community. A people that repudiates each past generation would lose its continuity, and remaining together would require that new bonds be established each time the past is repudiated. One form of the unity of a people is unity over time. This requires some link with the past as well as the future. The Mosaic covenant was unambiguous on this point. The moral obligation through which this was to be realized is to expect from community members some positive attachment and some sense of obligation to those who had made their lives possible.

But the devotion to life and to the perpetuation of a community was not considered a sufficiently stringent way in which to express the value of human life. It is one thing to bring life into being and to be grateful for life as a gift from others; it is another to put oneself under the obligation not to kill.[4] The Mosaic covenant requires that whatever we think of others and however they may delight or annoy us, we are not to kill them. Killing cannot be universally countenanced if a community is to survive as a community. To band together with people and as a people would be futile and self-defeating if there were no agreed-upon constraint against killing. As H. L. A. Hart has argued, the very fact of human vulnerability, the very fact that each of us has the capacity to kill and the susceptibility to being killed, makes it necessary to constrain our urge to kill.[5]

Killing, then, is of community-wide concern, and institutions designed to define when it is murder and morally unacceptable are to be expected. We see here an important difference between the duty not to injure and the duty not to kill. Only certain forms of injury are severe enough to warrant total community concern. The Mosaic covenant insists that killing is one such form of injury. Implied also by this injunction against killing is that life itself is to be seen as a right that each member of a community has that every other member of the community is obligated to respect. Not every form of injury will imply or generate institutional arrangements. Acts of killing do generate such institutionalization. Procedural justice and the courts in which these procedures are concretized are necessary to adjudicate claims arising from acts of killing.

Stealing likewise requires this kind of social intervention if neighbors are to be prevented from divisive accusations and vengeful disputes. Moreover, the nature and extent of such institutionalized, community-sanctioned, and formalized intervention is only possible in the context of defining property and ownership of property. What constitutes stealing will depend not only on notions of property but on the way in which economic associations are structured. In a money economy, money is something that can be stolen. Taking money from someone else is not necessarily wrong in itself, however. Whether or not it is called stealing depends upon the agreements that exist for monetary exchange. The reformer John Calvin was himself influential in gaining acceptance for the view that charging interest on loans is morally justified. But Calvin limited his approval of taking interest only to instances where the money borrowed was to be used to make more money. Calvin considered it morally wrong to take interest on loans where the money borrowed had to be used for necessities. In effect, Calvin considered it akin to stealing to take money from people who did not have enough of their own for sustaining life and health. Here we see how a change in the way in which money may be used leads to a change in what is considered the morally justified taking of money.[6] That there is such a thing as the taking of money or other forms of property in a morally unjustified way is what the injunction not to steal is meant to signify.

A constraint against stealing is a requisite for there being economic associations and cooperation at all. Economic exchange is impossible in the absence of some constraint on the accumulation of property and money by individuals or corporations, particularly where others are seriously or utterly deprived of economic necessities. As Freud pointed out, any group that is severely enough deprived by the society in which it finds itself will not long identify with that society and will not see its laws as binding.[7] In short, stealing in the form of economic deprivation is destructive of community; its constraint is requisite to the continuation of community. It is interesting to note that the ancient prophets of Israel, like Amos (2:4-7; 8:4-14) and Micah (6:8-16), for example, pleaded with their nation to heed its original pledge to the Mosaic covenant and constantly prophesied the destruction of the nation whenever the poor were being robbed and injustices against them perpetrated.

Just as stealing connotes a violation of the expectations of mutuality and fidelity in economic associations, adultery connotes a similar violation with respect to the marital covenant.[8] Indeed, the understanding of adultery as a form of covenant violation is especially apparent from the way in which prophets of Israel used sexual images to describe infidelity to the Mosaic covenant as such. False gods were sometimes portrayed as prostitutes who tried to seduce people away from faithful covenant relations with the one true God.[9]

In calling upon people not to bear false witness, we see again how the Mosaic covenant is couched in institutional terms. Though a universal prohibition against lying is presupposed, the injunction in which it finds its expression is concretely tied to the procedures of a court of inquiry. People are being asked not to lie in court. If lying cannot be prevented or at least diminished significantly in attempts to adjudicate disputes and rectify injuries, justice soon becomes a mockery. Just as the prophets of Israel emphasized the destructiveness of oppressing the poor, they also visualized a people as doomed if witnesses and judges could be bribed and could thus subvert procedural and substantive justice in the courts. (See, for example, Micah 7:1–4.)

So far, then, we have illustrated one of the most important ways in which the Mosaic traditions differ from most of those found in contemporary moral philosophy.[10] Its moral injunctions are stated in such a way as to affirm that certain fundamental social institutions or human associations are recommended, the destruction of which is considered to be morally wrong. Religious, legal, political, economic, and familial associations ought not to be undermined by acts or policies that destroy the very possibility of their nurture and perpetuation. No blueprint is given as to the exact form and nature of these social institutions. The Mosaic covenant is morally unpretentious in this respect, quite unlike utopias or utopian thought.[11] No dictates are laid down that would inhibit growth and change. Rather its primary concern is to constrain evil on the part of those who would undermine or decimate the formation and possibility of human community. Implicit within it is the recognition that the meaning of fidelity in human institutions and associations requires continuous reinterpretation.

Even so, the Ten Commandments are too concrete in form to

suit many philosophers who are quick to point out that bearing false witness, for example, is an act of lying, and there are many other ways outside the courtroom for lying to take place. From an ethical point of view, it seems obvious that one should identify every form of lying as a wrong-making characteristic and not just bearing false witness. One can agree with that and yet disagree that a general prohibition against lying should replace the prohibition against bearing false witness.

When Ross describes lying as one of the wrong-making characteristics of actions and one of our morally significant interactions, he has indeed isolated one of the prohibitions of the moral life.[12] The Mosaic covenant, however, without in any sense being in conflict with Ross at such a point, is concerned to specify institutional arrangements that are morally significant. Ross does us a highly significant service insofar as he identifies the moral principles on which Mosaic prohibitions are based. But Ross's principles do not provide a substitute for the Mosaic injunctions, for references to explicit forms of community life are left unspecified by Ross. Ideally, any complete account of the moral life would include an understanding of both the most universal forms of morally significant relations between neighbor and neighbor as well as the most universal, morally significant institutional forms of human association.

Although it is important to recognize the moral significance of all lying, it is equally important to underline the specific procedural and substantive necessity of truth for justice in the courts and to flag also the moral obligation to routinize such truth-telling procedures. No less important is it to the moral life of a community to call for structures that do not leave the adjudication of disputes and the rectifying of injuries to the injured parties who may not have the power nor the information to see that justice rather than sheer vengeance or hearsay is received by anyone accused of injuring someone. The court is an institution that, when dedicated to truth-telling, prevents the escalation of injurious actions within the community that would surely result from failures to test the veracity of accusations against one's neighbor.

At this point we can begin to see that the evils cited and prohibited by the Mosaic covenant involve obligations of the most stringent character. Lying in the courtroom is not tolerated at all. In fact, it is a crime for anyone to lie under oath in a court proceeding. In ordinary life we can find reasons to lie or to fail to tell the truth. Certainly other things being equal, it would generally be recognized that the obligation to try to save a life is more stringent than the obligation not to lie. To lie in court, however, is to undermine the moral justification for courts as such. Courts are supposed to discover the truth, deal fairly with everyone, exonerate the innocent, and discover the guilty, and in accomplishing all this, to do so more predictably than if each individual in a society were to deal with killing, stealing, and other forms of injury against persons on a purely individual basis. One could in fact argue that courts exist precisely because there is no better known or imaginable way to restrain fairly, without escalating injury, the various ways in which people harm one another, whether advertently or inadvertently. In small and rather simple groups where individuals are known to one another, trusted individuals can take on the functions of what in a more complicated society requires courts. But in that simple setting, the constraint against lying in the context of trying to establish guilt or innocence would still be a more stringent obligation than the general obligation not to lie. The most obvious reason for this is that lying in the context of trying to establish guilt or innocence also violates standards of fair and equitable treatment and may further victimize one who is innocent or further reward one who has already benefited from injuring others.

In chapter 3 we argued that moral principles are constitutive rules—that is, they are basic rules that are presupposed and that make possible at all the formulation of additional rules that we generate and discard in the course of ordering our lives. Similarly the very concrete evils prohibited in the Mosaic covenant are concerned first and foremost with identifying those acts that are destructive of human associations, for to destroy such associations is to render community impossible. In other words, certain human associations or institutions are requisite to there being any form of community or cooperative action among people. It is those actions that are destructive of such associations or institutions that are identified and declared to be morally wrong in the Mosaic covenant.

In most of the philosophical literature—and in this respect Ross and Frankena are not exceptions—these specific instances of evil are not explicitly discussed.[13] Where Frankena does take up the question of institutions, albeit rather briefly, he does not claim that any particular form of association is morally obligatory, nor does he identify evils associated with the destruction of institutions.[14] Indeed, neither he nor Ross gives us any specific indication as to what kinds of things count as injurious or evil, nor do they when speaking of the obligation not to inflict injury specify what injuries, if any, can be clearly identified as the ones we are most stringently obligated to refrain from inflicting. The Mosaic covenant, whatever its shortcomings, does at least clearly and fundamentally take on this enterprise. We learn from it that certain classes of actions such as killing and stealing are, as Bishop Robinson has so eloquently expressed it, "so fundamentally destructive of human relationships that no differences of century or society can change their character." [15] In making this statement, Bishop Robinson should not be misunderstood. He would be among the last to claim that stealing and killing are always wrong as such. Rather, stealing and killing are the kinds of acts that are always wrong-making in character; and the kind of wrong involved in these acts is, as we have been arguing, precisely such as to strike a blow at the very possibility of initiating, nurturing, and perpetuating human communities.

We should indicate that Frankena explicitly points out that human institutions should conform to and be guided by moral principles. Undoubtedly, moral philosophers and religious ethicists would agree to that general proposition. Nothing we have said diminishes the importance of identifying and specifying the moral principles involved in our decisions regarding what is right or wrong. We have introduced the ancient code of the Mosaic covenant, for which there are counterparts in other religions and cultures, in order to introduce the reader to those constraints upon evil that serve to safeguard associations and institutions requisite to making the moral life possible. As John Rawls has pointed out, the kind of love and socialization that takes place within the context of the family is requisite for the development of a sense of justice.[16] There may be other institutional arrangements possible for moral development, but none of them could substitute for some human relationships in which love is reciprocally experienced and adult models with which to identify are provided.[17] In short, it is not enough to know what is right-making and wrong-making at the level of moral principles. The human associations that make it possible to know what is right and wrong, to conform to what is right, and to avoid what is evil, need also to be identified so that the actions that would be destructive of them can be identified as morally wrong-making.

Now we can begin to see what is involved in the prohibition against killing. As in the instance of philosophers' substituting not lying for not bearing false witness, it is clear that a prohibition against injuring anyone is on the face of it a more universal constraint than the prohibition against killing. Here, too, there are all sorts of injuries that do not involve killing, and every act of killing can be seen as a species of injury. However, we should emphasize that every act of killing *can* be perceived as an act of injury, for surprising as it may seem to some of us, killing is not always seen in this way. Indeed, as we saw in chapter 4, Kohl considers it more evil to tolerate some forms of suffering than to kill.

Considering now what we have been saying about the various prohibitions of the Mosaic covenant, it seems fair to ask whether suffering of the kind Kohl has in mind has to be relieved, because if it does not, human relationships requisite to the possibility of sustaining human communities will have been attacked or impaired in some way. The injunction against killing is fairly readily identified with respect to its role in trying to avoid the destruction of human associations and relations. Whether suffering is clearly an evil in this sense or in any other sense is a matter of great debate. Whereas the moral traditions of Judaism and Christianity do not question killing as an evil, even under conditions where it is sanctioned, the status of suffering varies tremendously from context to context. We could, therefore, give some arguments for considering the relief of suffering under some circumstances as a very stringent obligation, but we could also give very strong arguments on the other side. Similarly, we could argue for the merit of certain forms of suffering—for example, pangs of conscience over an evil deed; and yet there are circumstances in which even such suffering cries out for relief although the method of relieving it may in turn be a matter of great debate. Suffering, like the notion of dignity, is a conception that in our contemporary world requires much analysis.

This short treatise on ethics is no place to begin that large task. We are content to make the simple claim that killing is much more readily identifiable as an evil we should stringently disavow, while suffering is something we may deem it good to relieve, but the stringency of the obligation to do so is not apparent.

We are at a very critical juncture in our society. It is a time when the special stringency of the injunction not to kill is being questioned, not only in thought, but also in deed. We see this in the area of infant care. Laws against child abuse have been developed and enacted throughout the United States. In accord with these laws, physicians and other professionals can exercise the power to remove from their homes children who are badly treated, who suffer severe physical and/or psychological abuse at the hands of their parents or guardians.[18] However, at this very moment decisions are being made at a number of medical centers that newly born infants who are diagnosed as mentally retarded or even potentially retarded may not be allowed to live. Thus, for example, some physicians like Duff and Campbell at Yale obtain the consent of parents not to engage in life-saving interventions of even very predictably successful kinds when infants are diagnosed as having Down's syndrome and therefore would be retarded, in some cases severely, but in some cases not so severely as to prevent them from being trainable or educable.[19] It should also be noted that children with Down's syndrome are generally acknowledged to be quite happy and emotionally responsive. Nevertheless, such children are the victims of decisions that take their lives. Whereas it is unthinkable that a physician should slap or strike or torture such an infant, it is not unthinkable, indeed it is increasingly being done, that a physician, consulting with parents or guardians, fails to provide life-sustaining interventions for some infants who are deformed in some way and who need special medical intervention such as surgery.

Someone may argue that there is such a thing as morally justifiable killing. And Mosaic traditions recognize this. Drawing on Mosaic traditions one can argue the moral justifiability of defending oneself against an aggressor. One can take life, as well as give one's life, in order to save life. But the value of human life as such is not questioned by such exceptions. The idea that life in itself is not worth the most stringent protection is foreign to Mosaic traditions. When taking a life is justified on the grounds that that life is not worth living, one of the moral requisites of community is undermined. All human beings are vulnerable, but infants are especially so. They cannot defend themselves. If a society withdraws its defenses of its most defenseless members, the question arises whether it is in the interest of persons to enter into covenant with such a society.

Hobbes once argued that the warrant for government is anchored in the defense it can provide for the lives of the individuals who form a society under its jurisdiction.[20] When a government is unable or unwilling to protect the lives of its citizens, Hobbes contended, those citizens should no longer feel obligated to obey and respect it. Indeed, Hobbes insisted that the right to self-defense is one that cannot, nor should not, be taken away by any government. If the king's men in Hobbes's day, or the police in ours, do not observe due process in arresting people accused of crimes, but simply without provocation seek to kill those they should arrest, Hobbes contends that in such instances people have a right to defend their lives. People who are too young, like infants, or too old or otherwise handicapped for whatever reason, have only the protection of life that is afforded by the larger society in which they are members. Take away the constraints against killing such defenseless people and you have taken away the most fundamental reason for being a member of a society. That is one reason why in the context of the Mosaic covenant it is killing, not just injuring, that is explicitly enjoined against. Unless a group agrees to a constraint against killing as such, the wisdom of becoming a member of that group is highly questionable, and the moral requisite of group cooperation and cohesiveness has not yet been obtained. When, for example, the euthanasia law in Germany was applied to all German citizens, the resulting widespread paranoia and distrust of the government caused the Nazi government to relent in its application.[21]

Blacks have always recognized the genocidal overtones implied by any assumption in the power structures of a community that some group or individual is for one reason or another less than human. The development of black power and the constant discussion of black nationalism reflect the understandable uneasiness that pervades a group that is uncertain about the equal protection of the right to live of the group and its members.[22] A society lacks a moral requisite of community if life as such is not honored as a value that all its members and potential members share, regardless of age, alleged competence, physical traits, and all the other contingencies of human birth and illness for which people cannot be held totally morally responsible.

At this point we see an important link between the value of life and justice. What we have been arguing for is not only that life be treated as valuable in itself regardless of its particular qualities but also for the presumption that all human beings ought to be granted equal right to and protection of their lives.

Equality is a central feature of justice. In the most thorough, recent study of distributive justice, John Rawls has underlined this conception of justice.[23] Justice as fairness incorporates two principles. The first is that there should be maximum liberty compatible with like liberty for all. In this principle, Rawls is arguing that there should be strict equality of human rights such as liberty. This type of equality is illustrated in our commitment within the courts to due process, to similar treatment of similar cases, and the like. It can also take the form of equality of opportunity, which is the expression that Frankena favors in arguing for justice as equality.[24]

In arguing for strict equality in the area of basic rights, Rawls does not exclude the possibility of justifying certain differences among people. But this, for him, is to be done in accord with the demands of justice as stated in his second principle:

> Social and economic inequalities are to be arranged so that they are both (a) to the greatest benefit of the least advantaged and (b) attached to offices and positions open to all under conditions of fair equality of opportunity.[25]

Questions of distributive justice are, of course, very complicated and quite beyond the scope of our more introductory volume. We have raised the question of justice in order to call the reader's attention to the significance of questions of justice for the protection of individuals against evil. In this respect, it is important to note the inadequacy of W. D. Ross's formulation of justice. Ross sees justice as the duty to rectify any distribution of pleasure or happiness that is not in accord with the merit of the persons concerned.[26] The word *merit* is what creates the most difficulty unless further clarified. Strictly speaking, there is nothing that anyone can do to earn or merit the right to life. All of us owe our lives to the actions of others. These actions include not only the initiation of life itself but also the kind of nurturance, cooperation, and restraint against inflicting evil that makes survival for any human being a reality. Even the most independent individuals imaginable are vulnerable in various ways—certainly while asleep or ill.

This brings us to one of the special ways in which physicians are involved in the question of justice. Health professionals are constantly making judgments about who is most in need of their services. For example, someone who risks dying is given what we call emergency treatment, and sometimes this means relative neglect of patients who are less immediately threatened by death. On the face of it, this is unequal treatment. But is it unfair or inequitable? I think it is safe to say that it is not. To treat those who are most threatened by death before treating those who are less threatened is to honor the presumption of a strictly equal right to life. If patients are to be treated as having an equal right to life, then those most in danger of dying will be cared for first. As Frankena has argued, the notion that justice is a matter of meeting needs, rests in the last analysis upon a notion of equal treatment. Those who are handicapped in some way will need extra attention to assure that they have as much in the way of equality of opportunity as those who are not handicapped.

However, when physicians or other health professionals decide that some individuals do not deserve lifesaving treatment because they are lacking in certain intellectual potential or achievement, they are undermining the principle of strict equality of life and liberty for every human being. They are invoking merit when it is unfair to do so. To note this is not to argue against merit theories of justice as such but, rather, to highlight some ways in which certain notions of merit would violate justice as a form of equality of treatment. At the same time, unequal treatment based on merit is clearly applicable in the area of criminal justice. Persons who have killed other human beings, for example, have forfeited their usual right to equal liberty and equal treatment. In order to maintain itself and uphold a strict injunction against unjustified killing, a society will be obligated to see to it that pleasure or happiness is associated not with murder but with the observance of constraints against murder and the desire to make up for such a wrong insofar as it is possible. Again it would take us too far afield to explore complexities of criminal justice. It is enough here to indicate that the idea of merit as a form of appropriate or deserved response to immoral actions does enter into questions of justice within that context. Thus we distinguish between guilty persons who "merit" some kind of punishment or special treatment and innocent persons whose rights to equality should not be jeopardized.

What if someone argued that, sure enough, we should not base decisions as to whether we should or should not save patients' lives on the basis of their personality, age, income, intelligence, and the like? However, are there not some characteristics of human beings on the basis of which they are to be counted as persons? Human beings who have these qualities of personhood are indeed entitled to strict equality of treatment and opportunity, but human organisms that lack certain characteristics deemed necessary for personhood are not entitled to such equal treatment. Those who argue in this way would differ considerably as to what these characteristics might be. Joseph Fletcher, for example, has argued that a Down's syndrome child is not a person.[27] In a somewhat later work, he argued that certain levels of intelligence, social interaction, and autonomy are requisites for being treated as a person.[28] Here the question of merit simply resurfaces in a new form. Attempts to define personhood are attempts to specify who among individuals who are somehow part of the human species qualify or do not qualify for the usual kind of equal protection against evil afforded to persons. Again, this is like the lawyer in the story of the Good Samaritan who feels compelled to ask, "Who is my neighbor?" The answer to that question was, "the Good Samaritan is one's neighbor." And if one asks who is a Good Samaritan, it is one who observes impartially all the constraints against evil found in the Mosaic covenant and shows mercy or compassion to one who without care would die. The merit of the patient who is cared for by the Samaritan is not up for discussion. Merit, however, is attributed to that loving Samaritan, and through the ages we have called that Samaritan good.

DOING GOOD AS A FORM OF NEIGHBORLY LOVE

What do we mean when we call someone a Good Samaritan? So far, we have examined part of what we mean: a Good Samaritan is someone who does not inflict evil on others. This is the moral principle, or duty, of nonmaleficence. The Mosaic covenant, as we have seen, suggests some of the most stringently obligatory forms of nonmaleficence, and we have tried to indicate some reasons these obligations are so stringent. Our discussion of evil does not presume to be complete, only suggestive.

The word *good,* however, is very much used in ethics, and moral philosophers and moral theologians generally include doing good, or beneficence, among the moral principles they are willing to recognize. We are not now speaking of beneficence in the form of preventing and removing evil but, rather, specifically in the form of doing good.

As we noted in chapter 3, utilitarianism has used good or goodness as the sole criterion by which to judge the rightness and wrongness of actions or policies. The formalists have contended that good and bad consequences are not the only criteria for judging rightness and wrongness. However, most ethicists retain, as one obligation among others, the obligation to do good, and certainly they want to recognize that the rightness or wrongness of actions or policies will depend at least in part on the goodness or badness of the consequences expected to issue from them.

Pleasure is clearly one of the states of being that a variety of ethicists over the centuries have claimed to be good. We need not repeat the difficulties of a utilitarian argument that pleasure is the sole criterion of rightness. Nonetheless, someone like W. D. Ross does treat pleasure as a good and includes under beneficence the obligation to bring about pleasure for others. (He assumes that we will continually seek pleasure for ourselves and posits no duty to do so.) [29] And even though Ross considers nonmaleficence a more stringent obligation than beneficence, is it not still problematic to introduce the conferring of pleasure on others as one of the right-making characteristics of actions?

Would it not be wrong and certainly not obligatory to endeavor to help someone experience pleasure over having committed some moral wrong? Imagine, for example, that a friend of yours has succeeded in deceiving someone and is feeling somewhat unhappy about it. Much as you might enjoy cheering up your friend, perhaps even by making jokes about the one whom your friend has deluded, would it be the case that you have a moral obligation to do so? Would it not be plausible to argue that it might even be wrong to assist your friend in being happy about his evil action, and if you have any moral obligation at all to turn your friend from unhappiness to happiness, it would lie in advising him as to how much better both of you would feel if he did something to make up for the wrong he had done if this were possible, and if not, to resolve not to deceive people in this way again? From this example, we can see that conferring pleasure on others is not by itself a right-making characteristic of actions, rather it would be right-making if such pleasure were morality supporting. To say that an act is morality supporting is to say that it contributes to doing what is right and refraining from what is wrong, while at the same time it is an act that does not violate any of our other moral principles. Here, Ross would agree since he considers nonmalefi-cence a more stringent obligation than conferring pleasure on others. Where we take issue with Ross, however, is in not treating pleasure as a good in itself. Pleasure at bringing about some evil or pleasure derived from the pursuit of evil is not something we can call good, nor can we call any act obligatory or right that helps us or others experience pleasure of this kind.

Some have questioned whether the conferring of pleasure, whether on ourselves or others, should be regarded as an obligation at all. The moral philosopher Bernard Gert has argued quite cogently that moral principles, or what he calls moral rules, are to be obeyed at all times with equal regard to everyone, and as he goes on to note, it is not only possible but fairly easy to obey moral rules all the time with regard to everyone equally. However, the rule "promote pleasure" is humanly impossible to obey all the time regarding everyone equally.

> These considerations are all very closely connected to the fact that all moral rules are or can be, with no change in content, stated as prohibitions on actions. Thus keeping these rules at all times with regard to everyone equally is accomplished simply by not breaking them at any time with regard to anyone. But the rule "Promote pleasure" demands positive action, hence the difficulty in following it at all times with regard to everyone equally.
>
> Moral rules require us not to cause evil for anyone; they do not require us to promote the general good.[30]

At first blush, the very idea that there should be no obligation to promote good seems like a denial of the whole moral enterprise. Yet every tyrant who has perpetrated great evils has done so in the name of some public good. There is no end to the range of things that people are willing to call good. Anyone who is suggesting that doing good is morally obligatory—that is, one moral principle among others—will need, at the very least, to specify carefully how the word *good* is being used in this context.

Frankena is among the moral philosophers who recognize the problematic character of positing doing good as a moral principle. Earlier, in chapter 4, he was cited as saying that it is plausible to question whether doing good is a moral obligation. One important reason for this is that the term *good* may be used in both moral and nonmoral senses. Frankena has defined these different senses in the following way:

> The sorts of things that may be morally good or bad are persons, groups of persons, traits of character, dispositions, emotions, motives, and intentions—in short, persons, groups of persons, and elements of personality. All sorts of things, on the other hand, may be nonmorally good or bad, for example: physical objects like cars and paintings; experiences like pleasure, pain, knowledge, and freedom; and forms of government like democracy. It does not make sense to call most of these things morally good or bad, unless we mean that it is morally right or wrong to pursue them. Partly, the distinction between judgments of moral and nonmoral value is also a matter of the difference in the *grounds* on or *reasons* for which they are made. When we judge actions or persons to be morally good or bad we always do so because of the motives, intentions, dispositions, or traits of character they manifest. When we make nonmoral judgments it is on very different grounds or reasons, and the grounds or reasons vary from case to case, depending, for example, on whether our judgment is one of intrinsic, instrumental, or aesthetic value.[31]

Frankena recognizes, of course, that something may be both morally and nonmorally good at the same time. For example, love of one's neighbor is a morally good disposition, but it is normally also a source of pleasure or happiness and so may be also called good in a nonmoral sense. We also distinguish between saying of persons that they "had a good life" and saying of these same persons or others that they "led a good life." When we say that someone led a good life, we are saying that it was for one reason or another a morally good or virtuous life. When we say that someone had a good life, we are probably referring to the fact that it was a happy or pleasurable life, and we are thus using *good* in a nonmoral sense, without in any way implying that such a life was immoral.

Readers who wish to pursue various theories of good in the nonmoral sense would find Frankena's discussion a helpful place to begin. He devotes a whole chapter to this and develops a list of nonmoral goods, including among them pleasure, truth, knowledge, beauty, power, experience of achievement, self-expression, and security.[32] It takes little imagination to visualize or recall the unspeakable crimes that have served people's quests for power, achievement, security, and self-expression. But knowledge, truth, and pleasure can also be used for evil ends or sought through evil means. In short, there is a serious question about whether there is a duty to do good over and above our clear duty to avoid, prevent, and eliminate evil.

On Frankena's view, whatever is good in the nonmoral sense is good because of the presence of one or both of two factors: pleasure or satisfaction on the one hand, and some kind of excellence on the other. Working, then, with those two concepts, namely, pleasure and excellence, we return to the question under discussion. Is there a duty to promote pleasure and excellence? The arguments we have already applied to pleasure apply as well to excellence. It is the appropriate kind of excellence that would be right-making. The perfect murder, for example, would be a form of excellence, but excellence in doing evil, which it could not possibly be a duty to promote.

Pleasure and excellence, however, are requisites for the moral life. If human beings were so constituted as to derive extreme pleasure only from doing evil and extreme pain only from fulfilling their obligations, such a world would from our present perspective be considered totally evil and unjust. To prevent such a world or, more realistically, to prevent instances of pleasure in doing evil and pain in fulfilling obligations, it would seem reasonable to confer pleasure on those who do what is right. We could accept, then, an amended version of Ross's principle of beneficence which would posit an obligation to confer pleasure that is morality supporting.

Ross includes intelligence or knowledge as another good that we are obligated to confer upon others. Here again, we would argue that it would be obligatory to confer on ourselves and others only such knowledge as would be morality supporting and not in violation of other obligations. At this point we encounter what appears to be a paradox. Perfect knowledge is, as we shall argue in more detail in chapter 7, a characteristic of an ideal moral judge and thus is morality supporting. Yet we are saying that there is no moral obligation to pursue knowledge as such, only an obligation to pursue knowledge insofar as it is morality supporting. This seeming paradox vanishes, however, when one considers that the characteristics of an ideal moral judge, whom one must suppose to be all-knowing, cannot be considered in isolation from one another. An ideal moral judge has a number of characteristics, and it is the combination of these characteristics that makes an ideal moral judge ideal. Someone with perfect knowledge but without feeling, for example, would not be an ideal moral judge.

So knowledge, like pleasure, is a nonmoral good we can all freely pursue provided that we do not perpetrate any evil in the pursuit of it. The point we are making here is quite in keeping with Gert's claim that "the promotion of good does not justify the infliction of evil; only the prevention of greater evil does that." [33] Gathering knowledge for ourselves and others does become morally obligatory when it is needed to prevent evil and/or to aid our discernment as to what in particular circumstances we are obligated to do, because then it is morality supporting.

BEING GOOD AS A FORM OF NEIGHBORLY LOVE

Ross's statement of the principle of beneficence includes one more good that he says we are obligated to try to bring about, namely, moral virtue. The expression *moral virtue* may be unfamiliar to readers or may have an unfortunate connotation. From the perspective of ethics, moral virtues refer to dispositions or character traits that are judged to be morally good.

As readers can well imagine, there has been much debate over what will count as moral virtue, and long lists of candidates have accumulated and could be cited. In Frankena's discussion of this, he comes to the conclusion that he is willing to consider as moral virtues those dispositions that incline us to fulfill our moral obligations. [34] Since within the context of this particular introduction to ethics we are recognizing, in amended form, a set of moral obligations articulated by W. D. Ross, we could then say that for each of these obligations there is a disposition to fulfill it, and each of these dispositions is a moral virtue. Thus, for example, it is our obligation to tell the truth, and the disposition to do so is a moral virtue. All these moral virtues may be summarized and stated more simply as moral conscientiousness, i.e., the disposition to do what is right or obligatory in any given instance. This is a disposition that has been uniformly accepted as a moral virtue by ethicists.

But there is at least one other disposition that deserves recognition as a moral virtue. The will to do what is right does not by itself lead to right action. Persons who fail or who have difficulty in discerning what is right may, despite their utter willingness to do what is right, end up doing what is wrong. Therefore, the disposition in the form of a sensitivity that helps us know what is right is also a moral virtue because it is a trait of character that is clearly morality supporting. In another context, we have called this moral virtue moral perceptivity. It is

the ability vividly to imagine, that is, both to feel and to perceive, what other persons feel and need, and how they are, or would be, affected by our attitudes and actions. This ability, when operative, informs our decisions as to whether there are moral claims upon us in a given situation, and if there are, which and how stringent. Thus, as one of the ways in which what is obligatory is revealed to us, this ability or sensitivity is an essential part of what we mean by our sense of obligation. Having a sense of obligation requires or entails having this virtue.[35]

Since moral virtues, then, are considered morality supporting in the sense of disposing people to do and to discern what is right, doing good in the form of helping others and ourselves to be and to become morally virtuous should be considered a moral obligation. Hence we are agreeing with Ross in recognizing as an obligation the encouragement in ourselves and others of the development of moral virtues. When we speak of individuals as Good Samaritans we are generally speaking of those who have certain character traits or dispositions that dispose them to fulfill their obligations, as well as to know what these are.

All too briefly, now, we have tried more nearly to specify the principles of nonmaleficence and beneficence. With respect to the principle of nonmaleficence, we have made use of the Mosaic covenant, and the special circumstances that gave rise to it, to argue the necessity for being specific about forms of evil that would be destructive of human associations and institutions requisite for human community and hence for the moral life. Such evils specify the most stringent forms of the principle of nonmaleficence. These are evils we are not to inflict on others, not even for the sake of doing good. With respect to beneficence, we have tried to show that doing good is only morally obligatory when it is morality supporting. An act is morality supporting if, and only if, it contributes to doing what is right and refraining from what is wrong, and is an act that does not violate any of our other moral obligations. Beneficence, then, as a moral obligation, insofar as it involves doing good, is the obligation to do what is morality supporting. This will include improving our own moral character and that of others. It will also include bringing about a whole range of nonmoral goods, but only when doing so can be construed as morality supporting.

But the principle of beneficence or of conferring benefits is not restricted to the notion of doing good. As we have noted before, we can also benefit people by preventing and removing injury or evil. The prevention and removal of injury or evil, unlike doing good, may sometimes be more stringent as obligations than the obligation of nonmaleficence. This occurs very often in medicine when it is decided that a person needs a particular surgical or other medical intervention. In cases where health professionals are deciding whether to inflict injury on persons (that is, whether to violate the principle of nonmaleficence), they precisely seek to determine whether the benefits in the form of preventing or removing some injurious condition outweigh the risks of injuring the patient through some intervention deemed to be medically efficacious and appropriate. According to our understanding of the principle of beneficence, we do not see this kind of medical intervention as a form of doing good in the strict sense but rather as a benefit in the form of either preventing or removing some existing injury or evil. For as we tried to argue earlier, inflicting injury cannot be justified in the name of doing some good but rather for the sake of preventing or removing some greater injury or evil. When, therefore, health professionals are weighing benefits against risks, benefits often have to do with the prevention or removal of injury or evil and risks are associated with the infliction of injury or evil. This point applies to decisions about therapy as well as decisions about research.

The principle of beneficence, then, as we have interpreted it has three components: benefiting ourselves or others in the form of doing good; benefiting ourselves or others in the form of preventing injury and evil; and benefiting ourselves or others in the form of removing injury and evil. Benefits in the form of doing good have to be morality supporting in the sense we have specified above. The prevention or removal of injury or evil may justify the violation of other moral obligations, including the most stringent obligation not to injure or inflict evil. The justification for recognizing certain things as morally obligatory or right has not yet been adequately dealt with and awaits the discussions in the chapters that follow.

Chapter V—Suggestions for Further Reading

Readers will find discussions of these issues in the books referred to at the end of chapter 1.

chapter vi
relativism

In the preceding chapter we have taken the view that there are classes of actions, such as killing and stealing, "so fundamentally destructive of human relationships that no differences of century or society can change their character." [1] But some readers may doubt or even dispute such a claim. Why? Because they believe morals are relative, varying over time, among persons, and across cultures.

What does it mean, however, to say that morals are relative? Sometimes espousals of relativism are made in such a way that it would seem hopelessly naïve or uninformed to deny the relativity of ethics and of moral judgments. For this reason alone, it is surely important in any introduction to ethics to try to gain some measure of clarity about the various ways in which people apply the word *relativism* to the subject matter and assertions of ethics.

That individuals and groups disagree in the application of ethical terms or that individuals and groups vary as to their moral evaluations is hardly a matter for dispute. What it amounts to is a simple *description* of certain facts about the moral life. Such facts include the wide variety of divergent opinions that one normally observes with regard to the rightness and wrongness of infanticide, euthanasia, capital punishment, and a whole host of issues too familiar and numerous to mention. Not only is there a contemporaneous clash of moral evaluations among individuals and groups, but individuals and groups also undergo changes over time, even reversals, with respect to what they consider morally acceptable. Theologians and philosophers alike assume that every ethical theory must in some way come to grips with the sheer fact that moral evaluations differ.

By itself, the assertion that moral evaluations are diverse does not constitute a commitment to a theory or a point of view that might appropriately be designated as relativism. In other words, relativism is a theory that offers some interpretation or explanation of the fact of moral diversity and, as such, it has been applied to at least the following four sorts of claims regarding the nature and scope of moral diversity:

1) That the application of ethical terms varies from situation to situation in such a way that there are no exceptionless moral rules (contextual relativism).

2) That individuals (groups) ultimately vary in the application of ethical terms (psychological relativism).

3) That ethical terms vary in meaning from speaker to speaker or group to group because they refer to the speaker who uses them or to that speaker's group (ethical relativism). Characterizing the meaning of ethical terms in this way implies that it is not logically contradictory for one individual (group) to assert that truth-telling, for example, is right and for another individual (group) to assert that it is wrong.

4) That no method unique to moral discourse exists for rationally justifying moral assertions (methodological relativism).

CONTEXTUAL RELATIVISM

Contextual relativism is found in the writings of some contemporary theological ethicists. Philosophical ethicists, as a rule, neither espouse this view nor speak of anyone who does as a relativist. Their use of the term *relativism* is usually reserved for what we have called *ethical relativism,* the view that ethical terms vary in meaning depending upon the speaker or the speaker's society. Thus, for example, the philosopher Charles L. Stevenson makes it very clear that it is ethical relativism

> that is of philosophical interest. It has no connection, of course, with the view that an action's value depends upon, and thus is "relative to," the circumstances in which it occurs; but that is as it should be, since the latter view tends to be shared by relativists and nonrelativists alike. Socrates, for instance, can scarcely be called a relativist, yet he took it for granted that the value of an act depended on the circumstances, as is evident from his remarks about returning a deposit of arms to a man who is not in his right mind. [2]

What, then, is the issue that arises for theological ethicists that leads them to make the sort of claim that we have called contextual relativism?

Theological ethicists, or at least quite a number of them, are eager to detach themselves from what they call absolutism. They find absolutism in both philosophical and religious ethics. In philosophical ethics, one of the favorite targets is Kant. Kant once expressed the view that one should never tell a lie, not even if the lie was intended to save the life of a friend. The implication of this analysis was that lying is always wrong, regardless of the circumstances. The theological ethicist Dietrich Bonhoeffer, reacting to this kind of absolutism, states categorically that ethics can offer us nothing exceptionless. Paul Lehmann explicitly characterizes the absolutist as one who believes in general, exceptionless rules. Lehmann, then, like Bonhoeffer, repudiates this kind of absolutism.[3] Both of these ethicists may therefore be characterized as contextual relativists.

In their attack on absolute or exceptionless rules, contextual relativists may be taking one or more of three positions:

1) that differences in situations affect and sometimes make for differences in the application of ethical terms;
2) that because of differences from situation to situation, it is not possible to state any moral rule or obligation in an exceptionless form;
3) that because of the variation in the application of moral terms from situation to situation, the application of ethical terms ultimately varies (psychological relativism).

If contextual relativists call themselves relativists simply on the ground that variations in situations can and to some extent will be reflected in variations in the way in which we use ethical terms and make moral judgments, then I think it is fair to say that everyone in ethics could appropriately be referred to as a contextual relativist. Indeed, Charles Stevenson, cited earlier, noted that ethical relativists and nonrelativists alike accept the notion that what is considered to be moral is "relative to" the circumstances in which a moral decision or an application of an ethical term is actually occurring. What we are saying, then, is that ethicists generally agree with contextual relativists regarding a certain expected variation in moral judgments from situation to situation, but that within philosophical ethics, one does not usually use the word *relativism* to describe this point of view. Insofar as theological ethicists use the term *historical relativism* to refer to contextual relativism as described in (1) above, ethicists generally, myself included, are historical relativists in this restricted sense.

But at least some contextual relativists seem to be making another kind of claim, namely, that it is not possible to state moral rules or principles in an exceptionless form. Certainly Bonhoeffer and Lehmann referred to above appear to be taking such a position, if not explicitly, then certainly by implication. In this particular form, I think that contextual relativism is failing, for whatever reason, to take into account that it is quite possible to distinguish between what W. D. Ross has called *"prima facie duties"* and "duty proper." Ross gives us the following account of this distinction.

> I suggest *"prima facie* duty" or "conditional duty" as a brief way of referring to the characteristic (quite distinct from that of being a duty proper) which an act has, in virtue of being of a certain kind (e.g., the keeping of a promise), of being an act which would be a duty proper if it were not at the same time of another kind which is morally significant. Whether an act is a duty proper or actual duty depends on *all* the morally significant kinds it is an instance of.[4]

Another way of characterizing this distinction between a prima facie duty or obligation and one's actual duty or obligation in any particular situation is to note that prima facie obligations like promise-keeping, truth-telling, reparation, gratitude, justice, beneficence, self-improvement, and nonmaleficence are right-making characteristics of actions. Insofar as an act has one of these characteristics, it would be right and obligatory to do such an act. However, as Ross indicates, when we are in a situation of making a moral choice, we are virtually always making a choice with regard to an action that has more than one right- or wrong-making characteristic.

In some of the simpler conflicts of duties or obligations, we sometimes find ourselves inclined to break a promise because the promise is relatively trivial and conflicts with a duty that is more stringent, given the circumstances.[5] For example, breaking a promise to be at a party in order to aid an accident victim and save a life would be one of the easier decisions to make when duties conflict because of the weighty claim of avoiding being an accessory to someone's death. One of the more difficult conflicts is the one we encounter when we feel obligated to injure or even risk killing someone in order to prevent the injury or killing of ourselves or someone else. In short, actions are morally complex, and it is not possible to state exceptionless rules in the form of "you should never break a promise," "you should never lie," "you should never injure anyone," et cetera. However, it is possible to say that promise-keeping is always a right-making characteristic of actions, injuring persons is always a wrong-making characteristic of actions, lying is always a wrong-making characteristic of actions, and so on.

Once one recognizes this kind of distinction between, on the one hand, right- and wrong-making characteristics of actions and, on the other hand, the contextual and morally complex character of any particular concrete action, we can see that the contextual relativist is making a valid point in complaining against simplistic generalizations that do not recognize the complex and contextual character of particular moral decisions. Whether a particular act of justice, of reparation, or of truth-telling is the right act in some particular set of circumstances is not something that can be stated in the form of an exceptionless rule. For example, the notion once held by Christians that taking interest is always wrong was questioned once a distinction was made between a situation in which borrowed money was used for necessities and a situation in which borrowed money was used to make money. As we noted in chapter 5, Calvin was morally opposed to charging interest on money that was borrowed and used for necessities, but he approved charging interest on money that was borrowed and used to make more money.[6] There is something to be said for recognizing this distinction today, but our point here is that the notion that taking interest is always wrong became, through changing circumstances, an untenable generalization. Taking interest was and can be judged as morally wrong when it is an act of injuring or otherwise taking advantage of someone who is already disadvantaged. However, taking interest when the money borrowed is used to make money can be morally justified.

But contextual relativists also do us a disservice when they make too strong a claim for a simple truth. Actual obligations—that is to say, actions that are morally obligatory in particular situations—do vary with circumstances and do so for good reason. It is not correct, however, to draw the conclusion from this that ethics can in no way state principles in an exceptionless form. As we have argued, there are morally significant relationships that can be stated in the form of characteristics of actions that are always right- or wrong-making.

Some theological ethicists will be unimpressed with our objections to contextual relativism. The price, they argue, of stating moral rules in an exceptionless form is that they are so general or abstract that they are virtually, if not totally, irrelevant to moral decisions. Joseph Sittler, for example, has taken this view,[7] and to support his contention, he cites an incident from the novel *The Cruel Sea*. The captain of a destroyer faces the dilemma of whether to drop a depth charge on an enemy submarine that he thinks is located immediately below several hundred men who have abandoned a torpedoed ship and who are waiting to be rescued. Fearing that he must destroy the submarine even if it means killing the survivors of the abandoned vessel, the captain observes that "one must do what one must do and say one's prayers."

Sittler believes that in this kind of instance, moral principles are irrelevant. What seems to support Sittler's case is that the weightiest prima facie obligation not to inflict injury on others—in this case, not to kill them—is presumably totally ignored or overruled. But is that true? On what grounds would a person conscientiously decide to do what this captain did? Clearly, no one would drop the depth charges simply in order to kill the men waiting to be rescued. To provide a moral justification for using depth charges that would kill these men, it is necessary to argue that destroying the submarine would save lives. The agony of the captain's decision can be seen as that of trying to ascertain with reasonable certainty that it is necessary to destroy the submarine as an act of self-defense—namely, as an act that will protect the lives of the men in his ship as well as the lives of the others who would be the target of the submarine if it would be permitted to escape. When the captain concludes that he must destroy the submarine despite the loss of the men waiting to be rescued, his decision implies that in his view the most lives will be saved by so doing.[8] On this interpretation of the captain's action, killing as a wrong-making characteristic of actions is not ignored but rather implemented under the most attenuating circumstances, circumstances in which saving life entails taking life. In short, we have here a rather unhappy version of self-defense. If moral principles were irrelevant to this situation, the captain would not need to speak about saying one's prayers, for there would be no reason to regret the loss of lives brought about by this action.

We would contend, therefore, that recognizing and formulating moral principles is not irrelevant, either for ethical theory or for actual moral decision-making. To specify clearly what kinds of actions "are so fundamentally destructive of human relationships that no differences of century or society can change their character" will help us avert moral tragedy.[9] Some of the witnesses in the Senate Watergate hearings reported experiences of moral tragedy. Some of them engaged in undercover activities that involved lying in order to keep these actions secret. These actions at the time were defended simply as necessary in order to achieve certain laudable goals. Now in retrospect, the destructive nature of lying and of secret, domestic surveillance became so evident to certain of these witnesses that they professed they would not now engage in those same activities. Such examples of moral tragedy indicate that it is all too easy to underestimate the practical import of what might seem to be a purely theoretical exercise, namely, that of thinking about the weight and significance of rules in the form of right- or wrong-making characteristics of actions.

At the same time, the practical import of situational factors is very evident to most of us. We easily overestimate the situational constraints on moral decision-making to the point of considering ourselves to be victims of circumstances. Some of our greatest admiration is reserved for those who make a moral decision to do what is right or best in circumstances where they could have failed to do so by declaring themselves to be victims of those circumstances. One need only recall instances, for example, of persons' having risked or suffered the loss of their employment by exposing some grossly unfair or dishonest act or policy on the part of their employers.

Some contextual relativists may have a further objection to stating any moral principles in an exceptionless form. Their ground for this may be the belief that the variation in the application of ethical terms from situation to situation is such that it extends also to actual genuine differences over the nature and scope of what we are calling moral principles. In short, contextual relativists may actually be psychological relativists, and we turn now to consider that particular form of relativism.

PSYCHOLOGICAL RELATIVISM

Psychological relativism is the theory that individuals (groups) ultimately disagree in the application of ethical terms or in their moral evaluations. The word *ultimately* here means that the differences in applying ethical terms extend at some point even to different or conflicting understandings and applications of our most basic moral beliefs, such as those expressed in the form of moral principles.[10] Psychological relativism is not, therefore, to be equated with the simple factual claim already noted that variation among moral evaluations does indeed exist. Psychological relativism is an *interpretation* of the data that document the diversity of our moral evaluations; and unless we do recognize its interpretative character, it would seem obviously true. It has seemed so to many social scientists, particularly students of ethnology. As we shall see later in this chapter, some have relied upon psychological relativism as a premise to make a case for their version of ethical relativism. It should be noted that the term *psychological* as used here does not mean that the observations and interpretations of the data as characterized by psychological relativists somehow stem from or belong to the field of psychology as such. The claim about human behavior and/or culture evolving from the doctrine of psychological relativism may be based on observations made by anthropologists, sociologists, or other social scientists as well.

Those who believe that moral evaluations do ultimately vary are assuming that the object being evaluated has the same meaning in all relevant respects for those whose moral evaluations are being compared. Psychologists Max Wertheimer and Karl Duncker have questioned this assumption, contending that it is not possible to assert any ultimate disparity in our moral evaluations until we ascertain the *meaning* of the contents to which those evaluations refer. Such evaluations cannot be compared in isolation from the situations that precipitate them, for what may appear to be different or even contradictory evaluations of the same situation may very well be evaluations of quite different situations. Wertheimer and Duncker, therefore, would question the assumption made by psychological relativists that those who favor infanticide and those who do not are reacting to an identical situation.[11] Duncker elaborates this very point in his analysis of infanticide.

Duncker has observed that descriptions of ethical diversity tend to give an oversimplified account of the context in which moral evaluations are shaped by describing only two of the components of such a context: the external situation or object (e.g., a newly born infant), and the diversity of behavioral responses to it. According to Duncker, psychological analysis requires that other aspects of the context be taken into consideration as well. A newly born infant may elicit pleasure in one parent and disappointment in another. These reactions are guided by how this infant is seen or interpreted, whether as an answer to one's desires or as an actualization of what was not desired. In actuality, then, two such situations are not as similar as they might appear to be. Duncker suggests, therefore, that in analyzing situations or objects that have value character, we must consider: (1) the externally given conditions; (2) the meaning of those conditions for the actor or speaker; (3) the moral beliefs experienced; and (4) the resulting actions or attitudes. It is Duncker's contention that psychological relativists point to the lack of constancy in the relation between aspects (1), the externally given conditions, and (4), the resulting actions or attitudes, and fail to recognize that the differences observed with respect to (4) may be due to differences with respect to (2), the meaning of a given situation for the actor or speaker.

Suppose two cultures A and B are said to possess ultimately different moral evaluations, because A permits infanticide and B does not. When we investigate the matter further, we discover that A sanctions the killing of infants only in the first few days of life. (Asch reports that infanticide, when practiced, generally occurs only during the first few days of life.[12]) Furthermore, in culture A the infant in the first few days of life is seen to lack qualities XYZ; and killing living creatures having characteristics XYZ constitutes a morally wrong act for both cultures A and B. Once the infant is old enough to have certain human characteristics attributed to it, the sanctions against killing it obtain in culture A as they do in B. Culture B views infants as possessing XYZ from the moment of birth, and so its prohibitions against killing them apply to the very first days of life as well. On Duncker's thesis, the difference in the moral evaluations of those who believe that infanticide is wrong and those who believe that infanticide is right does not constitute an ultimate difference in moral evaluations or principles. The disparity between the two moral reactions to infanticide stems from the diverse way in which the first few days of infancy are interpreted.

Duncker raises serious doubts concerning the doctrine of psychological relativism—the doctrine that individuals or groups ultimately disagree with one another with respect to the moral evaluations they make—for in the light of his analysis of infanticide and other cases of that sort,[13] it is difficult to see how one could conclusively show that people really do ultimately disagree with one another in any of the instances in which their moral evaluations differ. Of every apparent moral disagreement, it is possible to claim that a disagreement concerning the interpretation of nonmoral matters is involved. At the very least, therefore, Duncker has made it clear that unanalyzed examples of diverse moral practices, like those connected with infanticide, will not by themselves constitute evidence in support of psychological relativism.

Duncker's complete argument against psychological relativism rests on a much stronger claim, namely, his thesis that there is an invariant relation between moral evaluations and "situational meaning." According to Duncker,

> the same act, being the same with regard to all meanings involved, has never been observed to incur different valuations. That is to say: within the same pattern of situational meanings only one of two contrary behaviors can lay claim to the same ethical quality and valuation.[14]

Thus, for example, for any one culture's homogeneous pattern of interpreting infants in some single set of circumstances, between the two actions of "killing an infant" or of "letting it live," only one will be perceived and judged to be right.

Duncker is contending, then, that the relationship between our interpretation of nonmoral matters and our moral evaluation of them is such that, when individuals (or groups) agree on their nonmoral perceptions of and beliefs about X and on the total situation or context within which they see the occurrence of X, they will agree in their moral evaluations of X; and when individuals (or groups) disagree as to their nonmoral perceptions of and beliefs about this same X and its context, they will disagree as to their moral evaluations of X. Also, for any individuals (or groups), a change in their nonmoral percepts and beliefs about X and its context will lead to a change in their moral evaluations of X. This thesis, or, as Duncker would say, "this [heuristic] principle of ethical invariance," is a psychological doctrine standing in opposition to the doctrine of psychological relativism.

It is worth noting the unique and thorough attempt made by the philosopher Richard B. Brandt to prove conclusively that psychological relativism is true. Based upon his own painstaking study of the Hopi, Brandt purports to have found at least one kind of practice, causing harm to animals, that ultimately differentiates the moral evaluations of the Hopi from those of our own culture. Hopi children, for example, are permitted to play with birds and bring about their death by various means, including starvation and mutilation. Brandt further believes that the evidence strongly suggests in this case that no differences exist between the Hopi and ourselves with respect to nonmoral beliefs. The Hopi seem to be aware of suffering on the part of birds that are being mutilated, although Brandt is uneasy about whether this assumption is correct.[15]

Has Brandt managed to supply at least one example that sufficiently "proves" the truth of psychological relativism and, at the same time, "disproves" Duncker's alternative to it cited above? Apparently, he is not himself entirely willing to claim that much. For, as he says, "we must admit the case is not definitely closed."[16] Brandt seemingly recognizes the difficulty of being certain that he has adequately taken into account all of the relevant nonmoral beliefs about animals. Everything considered, Brandt, like some anthropologists, views the "evidence" for psychological relativism as more compelling than the "evidence" against it. But it seems more likely that the "evidence" either for or against psychological relativism is simply inconclusive.

Proving that either psychological relativism or Duncker's thesis of psychological invariance is true presents practical difficulties of such magnitude that it is difficult to foresee how one could accomplish such a feat. Anyone trying to provide such proof would have to be able to know with certainty all the nonmoral beliefs that are relevant in a specific case in which two moral judgments are being compared.[17] In principle this probably means that one would have to know everything whatsoever in order to separate relevant from irrelevant nonmoral beliefs. Furthermore, one would have to assume that there is sufficient agreement possible on a method of distinguishing the nonmoral from the moral so that parties to the dispute about the truth of psychological relativism or psychological invariance could agree in a given case about what beliefs are nonmoral.

Suppose, then, that one either rejects psychological relativism or at least does not believe that it is possible to assert its truth. In neither of these instances does one thereby deny the continuing existence of differences among individuals and groups regarding the rightness or wrongness of specific actions or policies. Indeed, one may also expect, even though one does not accept psychological relativism as true or as provable, that even the most conscientious and astute thinkers may continue to differ with respect to what moral beliefs and how many will count as basic moral principles. Even someone who believes in Duncker's thesis of psychological invariance can take the view, and probably would take the view, that there is no reason to expect that people will be sufficiently alike in their thinking and in their nonmoral beliefs to bring about complete agreement on practical and theoretical moral issues. If this is so, why then spend so much space and effort to try to convince the reader that it is not rationally warranted to believe in the truth of psychological relativism?

We come back, then, to a point made earlier, namely, that psychological relativism is a certain interpretation of the fact that people differ with respect to their moral beliefs. If psychological relativism were true or could be proved to be true, then it would be true that at least some moral disagreements would be ultimate in the sense that there would be no way in principle to expect or procure agreement for such disagreements. In effect, it would be futile to try to settle any moral disagreement or difference that could be called ultimate. From a practical standpoint, therefore, a belief in psychological relativism can serve to discourage individuals and groups from trying to resolve moral disputes. Indeed, as we shall see later, psychological relativism may be one of the reasons people have for arguing that it is possible to consider contradictory moral statements to be equally true (ethical relativism). Psychological relativism may also for some lead to skepticism with respect to the possibility of finding agreement in characterizing the nature of moral language, and hence, lead to skepticism with respect to the possibility of deciding whether any ethical theories, including theories of ethical relativism, are true or false. In short, psychological relativism can be used as a basis for skepticism concerning moral judgments and ethical theories.

We should not take lightly these tendencies that flow from a belief in psychological relativism. As the reader surely has experienced, there are those who will argue for irreconcilable differences among groups. The whole point of ethics is precisely to try to indicate ways in which people can avoid harmful and violent attempts to resolve conflict. There are, of course, various ways to deal with irreconcilable differences, but among the ways that have so far inevitably accompanied human conflict are numerous forms of organized and unorganized killing. As Hobbes has argued, individuals and groups are in a state of war, with their lives in jeopardy, until they agree to organize themselves to prevent killing. To do this a group will agree that life is desirable, and killing wrong, to the point of specifying under what circumstances killing will be both morally wrong and punishable. If two groups see themselves as ultimately differing with regard to moral principles or with regard to the value placed on human life, the motivation for peaceful relations and fidelity to peace treaties will be seriously undermined. The quest for peace, in other words, is precisely the search for some expected mutual desire to live and let live based on a belief or presupposition that some measure of tolerable agreement exists or can be found regarding the value of human life and of the variety of groups in which it is protected and fostered. Ethics tries to provide a basis for affirming and negotiating such values. Psychological relativism has the practical effect of undermining the very basis of the enterprise of ethics as well as of practical political accommodations and alliances. Only when Romans and Greeks, for example, realized that other cultures might have values somewhat like their own did the legal and moral basis for international trade become articulated and put into practice.

As we have indicated above, psychological relativism may lead people to affirm ethical relativism. We turn now to examine how this may occur.

ETHICAL RELATIVISM

Sociologist William Graham Sumner and anthropologist Ruth Benedict are among those who have perceived a great variation across cultures with respect to what kinds of things are identified as right and wrong, good and evil.[18] They espoused what we could appropriately call social relativism. It took the form of claiming that "X is right" means "X is in accord with the mores of my group." This theory implies that it is not a contradiction for someone in a particular group, A, to maintain that some specific act is right, and for another group, B, to maintain that the very same act is wrong. On such a view, moral statements do admit of truth or falsity in the sense that it is possible to verify empirically whether a particular moral assertion is or is not in accord with the mores of one's own group. However, in cases of conflicting moral judgments, there is no way to claim that one group or the other is closer to the truth when the two groups are both making their judgments in accord with their own mores. Anyone holding such a theory would have to say of any disagreement between contending parties that what is true for one person's group may not be true for some other person's group. Thus, for example, infanticide was right for Romans but wrong for Jews and Christians.

How plausible is this characterization of the meaning of moral terms? To ascertain this, we will need to examine the following premises on which it appears to be based:

1) If groups or societies disagree with one another in the application of ethical terms, then those terms vary in meaning from society to society.

2) Groups (societies) disagree with one another in their application of ethical terms.

3) Therefore, ethical terms vary in meaning from society to society.

Therefore, "X is right" must be interpreted to mean "X is in accord with the mores of my group [society]."

Expressed in this form, the logic of the arguments is impeccable, but are the premises and conclusion as such plausible? Looking first at premise (1), we can see that it is not necessarily the case that disagreement between two groups in applying ethical terms implies that those terms mean something different for those two groups. Given the knowledge that we now have, and given also the specificity of the definition of roundness, the quarrel between Columbus and his friends on the one side and his opponents on the other as to the roundness or flatness of the earth in no way leads us to conclude that roundness is an ambiguous term in the sense of having more than one meaning. It was true then as it is now that whether or not the earth is in fact round does not depend upon what group of people are asserting its roundness, but rather depends upon an investigation of the earth by means of which it can be proved that anyone who says the earth is flat is uttering a falsehood. In short, disagreement between groups does not logically imply ambiguity.

However, someone may argue that ethical terms are not like roundness and flatness. Whereas roundness and flatness have an agreed-upon meaning in terms of which facts may be gleaned to determine whether a specific person or group is properly applying those terms, disagreement with regard to the application of ethical terms may not be a reflection of factual disagreement. Someone who wants to make this point will have to base it not on the premise that two groups are disagreeing with respect to the application of ethical terms, but rather that they ultimately disagree in the sense that no further investigation of facts will completely suffice to procure agreement in the application of ethical terms. Premise (1) would have to be modified, then, to read: If groups or societies ultimately disagree with one another in the application of ethical terms, then those terms vary in meaning from society to society. Although this premise would now be a plausible one, it is highly problematic in at least two important respects.

First, it necessitates belief in the truth of psychological relativism for the purposes of both premise (1) and premise (2). As we have indicated earlier, however, it is difficult if not impossible to prove the truth of psychological relativism.

A second difficulty with this reformulation of premise (1) is that it may well be the case, although difficult if not impossible to prove, that individuals or groups ultimately vary with regard to their factual beliefs and that the data needed for definitive or total agreement on factual matters, as these are relevant to our application of ethical terms, may never be complete. This, then, is a problem as well for premise (2). Whether infanticide is right or wrong, for example, may be due to a disagreement with respect to whether infants in the first two years are seen as having the characteristics requisite to personhood rather than a disagreement as to whether killing innocent persons is wrong as a general rule. In order to prove that a disagreement between groups has to do with a difference in understanding ethical terms rather than nonethical terms describing infants, one would have to prove the truth of psychological relativism, and so far no one has been able to do so.

The conclusion of the theory—that is, that ''X is right'' means ''X is in accord with the mores of my group,'' is not one that seems to square with our understanding of moral discourse. It can make sense to say that X is right and yet not in accord with the mores of my group. Nevertheless, according to the social relativists, it should be self-contradictory to make this claim. When Luther challenged the mores of his Roman Catholic group, it did not seem to be a contradiction in terms to claim that certain things his group was doing were wrong; and yet they were certainly in accord with the prevailing mores of that group. Of course, a social relativist could argue that Luther then became a member of another group, as indeed he eventually did. This leads us to another consideration: What shall we call our group or society? Is my own family my group? If so, may it not be sensible to say that something I am doing is right even though it is not in accord with the mores of my family?

Sumner himself appears to have some doubts about completely identifying rightness with the mores of one's group because he sometimes speaks of ''rising above the mores.'' In the end, he may share the rather widely held belief that there can be and indeed should be occasions on which we reject what the mores dictate on the grounds that to act in accord with the mores would be wrong. It would not be hard, for example, to have people agree that certain policies of the Nazis, such as the extermination of the Jews, were in accord with the mores of that group and yet called upon group members to do something that was morally wrong.

Social relativism may be confusing the moral uses of the word *right* with the application of this same term to nonmoral considerations, such as manners or customs. One use of the term *right,* therefore, in this nonmoral sense is to say that a particular thing is not done in France, but it is in Spain; so it is *right* in Spain but *not right* in France. Table manners, for example, may vary from one society to another without involving any moral issues.

Having raised grave doubts about the plausibility of social relativism as a theory regarding the nature of moral discourse, we are not thereby denying the significance of the influence of the mores of the social groups with which we identify. There is no question that our ethical beliefs and behavior are, as Sumner and Benedict astutely observed, very much affected by the mores. The nature and extent of such influence, however, has to do with the causal analysis of the factors that help explain some of the reasons for our particular ethical beliefs and behavior.

There is another form of relativism formulated by the philosopher and sociologist Edward Westermarck.[19] Westermarck's theory is a type of personal relativism. For Westermarck, the claim that "X is wrong" means that "X would produce an emotion of moral disapproval in me if I were impartial and if I were aware of all the facts."

How does Westermarck make a case for this metaethical theory? His argument is difficult to formulate but probably is as follows:

1) Whenever someone says "X is wrong," that person tends to have an emotion of moral disapproval of X.
2) The most adequate explanation of premise (1) is that moral judgments are judgments about the speaker's emotions of moral approval and disapproval.
3) Therefore, to say that "X is wrong" is to say that "I tend to feel an emotion of disapproval toward X."

The first premise of this argument is not one that could be easily contested. It is surely at least in part true. It is premise (2) that is questionable. Our tendency to have an emotion of moral disapproval toward something that we consider to be wrong need not be explained in the way in which Westermarck does it. The following three explanations are at least equally plausible:

1) The emotion we feel is because of the judgment we make; the judgment causes the emotion.
2) The emotion influences the judgment.
3) The emotion is the datum or evidence on which is based the judgment of what is being approved or disapproved.

Any one of the above alternatives to Westermarck's second premise would, if true, refute Westermarck's theory. But why would one question Westermarck's theory and wish to explore others resting on different assumptions? First, to the extent that we are impartial and willing to be fully informed, it is not plausible to think of moral judgments simply as judgments about our own emotions. When we conscientiously judge something to be right or wrong, we do not usually see ourselves as making a judgment about ourselves, certainly not exclusively about ourselves and our own emotions. There are alternative ways of characterizing what it is that moral judgments refer to, and we should investigate such alternatives before accepting a theory like Westermarck's. Indeed we will do so in chapter 7.

Like social relativism, Westermarck's theory implies that it is not contradictory for one person morally to disapprove of X and for another morally to approve of it. This implication of Westermarck's theory provides a second reason for questioning it, namely, that there is at present no evidence for assuming or concluding that persons ultimately disagree in the application of ethical terms. There is no *a priori* reason, therefore, for denying the possibility of nonrelativist metaethical theories that would provide methods or a set of criteria that would at least in principle provide a basis for agreement in the application of ethical terms. As we shall indicate in the next chapter, such theories exist and are plausible. Now, however, there is still one more form of relativism to consider.

METHODOLOGICAL RELATIVISM

The claim of methodological relativism is that no method unique to moral discourse exists for rationally justifying moral assertions. In other words, ethics, or disciplined reflection on moral discourse, cannot provide a rational method for resolving disputes between two individuals (groups) who disagree as to what is right or wrong or who disagree as to the meaning of ethical terms. Methodological relativism presupposes not only that individuals (groups) ultimately vary in the application of ethical terms but also that ethical theories ultimately vary. In its most extreme form this claim would end in skepticism. In a less extreme form, the methodological relativist may be claiming that from the point of view of some scientific frame of reference, ethics emerges as a nonscience without the typical scientific canons of evidence or proof by means of which to test the truth or falsity of its assertions. Why would anyone become a methodological relativist, and how sound are the reasons that might be given for subscribing to this point of view?

To begin with, a methodological relativist assumes that psychological relativism is true. This, as we have already argued, is an assumption that cannot be proved or at least has not been proved. Hence, one of the major reasons for being a methodological relativist is suspect. Of course one could, as we indicated, be an utter skeptic with respect to rationality in ethics. There is no need to repeat here the moral as well as rational difficulties of such skepticism since these have been skillfully explored elsewhere.[20]

The temptation to move toward methodological relativism may be occasioned by a false view of science and of the relation between science and ethics. One may affirm methodological relativism because one assumes that knowledge or rationality in the sciences proceeds from proven assumptions. This, however, is surely a very unsophisticated and uninformed view of science. All scientific knowledge depends upon inductive and deductive processes, the truth of whose premises has not been proved. For when we are asked to prove the most fundamental assumptions of logic, whether used in the context of the natural sciences or ethics, we can only reply as did Aristotle, "By what logic?"

A more serious reason for thinking of ethics as something quite unlike scientific disciplines that yield empirically verifiable knowledge is the belief that ethics deals with moral experience; and moral experience, unlike experience with objects, never provides evidence for anything that is real or that lends itself to scientific validation. But there is no *a priori* reason for rejecting without examination theories that purport to identify those components of moral experience that do provide an empirical basis for moral beliefs and ethical theory. As Brandt has indicated, it may be that some social scientists are methodological relativists by default: they simply do not know about empiricist types of metaethical theories of the sort we shall be examining in our next chapter.[21]

Methodological relativism is not a position that has been

defended by any major theorist in ethics.[22] As we have attempted to show, none of the reasons examined that might prompt someone to be a methodological relativist appears to be particularly plausible. Perhaps one further practical reason some favor one or more of the forms of relativism discussed above deserves mention—namely, that some might consider it morally responsible to hold such a view. Why? Because it is seen either as a requisite for or as an expression of tolerance for the moral beliefs of others; or perhaps more accurately, those who are not methodological, psychological, and/or ethical relativists are seen as intolerant. The merits of tolerance we do not question; any of these forms of relativism as supportive or expressive of tolerance we do.

When tolerance refers to a tendency to live and let live, it may well be the case that methodological and psychological relativists alike are psychologically tipped in this direction by their assumption that "one moral belief is as reasonable or as good as another" or that there is no justifiable reason for trying to change or take issue with the moral beliefs of others. But only ethical relativism, if it could be proved true, would be in a position to justify the claim that one moral belief is as correct or morally good as another. However, like methodological and psychological relativism, ethical relativism does not provide a justification for changing or not changing particular moral beliefs held by individuals or groups. For this reason, these relativists cannot, unless they deny their theories, claim that individuals or groups have a moral obligation to adopt an attitude of live and let live.

If, for example, I were a psychological relativist taking the view that individuals (groups) ultimately vary as to how they apply moral terms and hence with respect to what they identify as moral obligations, the obligation to live and let live is not one that I can expect all individuals or all groups to share. On what grounds, then, could I hold someone obligated to adopt an attitude on which there is ultimate disagreement? Certainly I would have to make some claims beyond those of psychological relativism to give anyone who disagrees some basis for agreeing with me.

And if I were a methodological relativist, I would deny that there are any rationally compelling reasons why I should adopt one moral attitude rather than another. As a methodological relativist, I would have no method for claiming that it is reasonable to assert a moral obligation to live and let live, nor would I have a theoretical basis for morally condemning intolerance.

Lest we think that these examples are purely hypothetical, the following statement on human rights published by an executive committee of the American Anthropological Association should give us pause: "Respect for differences between cultures is validated by the scientific fact that no technique of qualitatively evaluating cultures has been discovered."[23] This appears to be an espousal of methodological relativism or at least would incline one toward such a view.

Tolerance, or respect for the moral beliefs of others, can also have another meaning, i.e., that in the moral sphere, respect implies that the views of others are taken seriously. Psychologically, methodological, psychological, as well as ethical relativists may very well be inclined to an attitude of indifference rather than respect toward the moral beliefs of others. To be merely "tolerated" in this sense is in itself sometimes a source of outrage. It can be seen as basically disrespectful. Nothing was more infuriating, for example, to those who protested the war in Vietnam, or to those who defended it, than the attitude of those who claimed neutrality or indifference or who acted as though one view of the war was as reasonable or good as another. As we have already indicated, methodological, psychological, and ethical relativism do not in themselves provide grounds for considering all individuals (groups) morally obligated to practice tolerance, whether as respect or as indifference, though people who hold these theories may exhibit one or the other of these attitudes.

At this juncture the reader may be less concerned about the relation of relativism to tolerance and much more concerned about the potentially problematic relationship of nonrelativism to tolerance, particularly to intolerance. This we will explore in our final chapter.

Chapter VI—Suggestions for Further Reading

Discussions of relativism are scattered throughout the books referred to in chapter 1.

chapter vii
the quest for the ideal moral judge

Although the mainstream of moral philosophy resisted the various forms of relativism already discussed, it was still at a very critical juncture as it entered the twentieth century. Increasingly it seemed unclear that judgments of what is right or wrong, good or evil, yielded knowledge about the real world, so that latent forces toward removing the field of ethics from the realm of knowledge began to become much more persistent and pervasive. These forces were associated with developments in science and in moral philosophy itself.

With the emergence of the modern sciences against the background of medieval thought, the place of value and value judgments in the empirically knowable world appeared to be increasingly jeopardized and sometimes utterly denied. The twentieth-century philosopher G. P. Adams has described this process and the kind of assumption often made within the sciences which is responsible for it.

> The world of nature, life, and mind was discovered to contain an infinite wealth of facts which could no longer be pressed into the older, simple teleological framework of values and of the Good. The inevitable and fruitful result was the growth of the physical, biological, and historical sciences bent solely upon the discovery and mastery of the facts of nature and of life, a cognitive enterprize which would have been impossible had it been guided by the older traditional assumptions of the fusion of reality and value. But there resulted as well just that insistent dilemma with respect to the basis of our practical interests and our judgments of value, a dilemma which has its roots in the assumption that orderly knowledge and science deal only with matter of fact, which is *wertfrei,* stripped of all . . . value, and that the world of our practical interests and values has its roots in will-attitudes, desire, and feelings totally distinct from our cognitive apprehension of the real. On these premises values . . . belong to a dimension and realm apart from that order of facts which may be known by scientific and theoretical inquiry.[1]

In this passage, Adams himself reflects some of the assumptions about the necessity or desirability of separating so-called facts from values. The eminent philosopher Bertrand Russell clearly shared this particular form of empiricism and the scientific ethos that engendered it, when he emphatically asserted:

> Ethics differs from science in the fact that its fundamental data are feelings and emotions, not percepts. This is to be understood strictly; that is to say the data are the feelings and emotions themselves, not the fact that we have them. The fact that we have them is a scientific fact like another and we become aware of it by perception, in the usual scientific way. But an ethical judgment does not state a fact; it states, though often in a disguised form, some hope or fear, some desire or aversion, some love or hate. It should be enunciated in the optative or imperative mood, not in the indicative.[2]

One of the distinct effects of this kind of thinking was to make many people skeptical that moral assertions could be anything more than private or personal opinions fueled by emotion rather than reason.

Writing at the beginning of the twentieth century, the philosopher G. E. Moore took very seriously this distinction between moral judgments and judgments of matters of fact issuing from science and philosophy.[3] More than any other philosopher, Moore began the modern enterprise of metaethics and provided much of the framework within which contemporary metaethical thinking takes place. Beyond the task of identifying the right- and wrong-making characteristics of actions and what kinds of things and persons will count as good and evil, he saw another enterprise for the field of ethics. In his view it was necessary to answer the question as to what a word like *good* means. Is it a word that can be defined? And if not, what kind of word is it? What is it that statements asserting the rightness or goodness of something refer to? Moore felt that if this question were answered, then we would know what kind of knowledge, if any, is provided by moral statements. And if one knew that, then presumably one would know how and the extent to which moral assertions can be justified, whether in the way scientific judgments are justified or in some other way.

Under Moore's tutelage, then, metaethics was launched as an explicit investigation of the nature of moral discourse. Before Moore, the distinction between normative ethics and metaethics had not been made explicit, nor was the question of justifying moral judgments focused on discovering the meaning of ethical terms.

INTUITIONISM

G. E. Moore was an intuitionist in ethics. Although he was by no means the first or the only intuitionist among ethicists, it was his particular arguments for intuitionism that not only influenced other subsequent intuitionists but also helped shape the way in which people formulated alternative metaethical points of view.

In the nineteenth century it was John Stuart Mill who provided the most popular alternative to eighteenth-century notions of intuition. Moore, however, directly attacked what Mill had set out to do. As we noted in chapter 3, Mill took the view that pleasure is the only thing that is good and pain the only thing that is evil. To decide whether or not a given action or policy is right or wrong is to decide whether the consequences of implementing that action or policy would result in more good than evil. Moore did not quarrel with Mill with respect to whether the rightness or wrongness of actions is determined by the extent to which such actions have good consequences. In fact, as we saw in chapter 3, Moore came under attack by W. D. Ross precisely because of his acceptance, though with some refinements, of this normative aspect of Mill's utilitarian theory. What Moore did object to in Mill, however, was what he took to be the suggestion that pleasure defines what is good. In other words, Moore took Mill to be saying that if you ask what the term *good* means, the answer is pleasure.

Setting aside the commonly held opinion that Mill did not really intend to define the term *good* by making it identical with *pleasure,* but only to identify pleasure as the right-making characteristic of actions and policies, let us consider now what problem Moore saw in attempts at such definitions. Moore claimed that you could never define a moral term like *good* by reference to some empirical characteristic of the world. Against anyone who takes the view that pleasure is the defining characteristic of goodness, it can be argued that it is perfectly sensible and logical to ask whether any particular act or policy that brings pleasure is good. Against certain philosophers who would define what is good by identifying it with what is desirable, it can similarly be alleged that it is sensible and logical to ask whether what is desirable is good. I might, for example, find it pleasurable and desirable to lie my way out of an embarrassing situation, but would it be true by definition that what I had done could be called good in any moral sense of the term? This simple test devised by Moore to expose any attempts to identify good with some empirical quality of the world has come to be known as the open-question test. Those who try to define *good* by reference to some empirical characteristic were accused by Moore of engaging in a "naturalistic fallacy."

Moore did not draw any skeptical conclusions from his attack on attempts to find empiricist definitions of moral terms. Rather, he believed that moral assertions referred to distinctive non-natural characteristics of reality known only by reason. Our ability to know what is good rests on intuitive or self-evident judgments made by reason. Moral assertions, therefore, can be judged to be true or false depending upon whether they satisfy our rational intuitions.

W. D. Ross accepted what for him was the cogency of Moore's objections to all attempts to identify terms like *right* and *good* with empirical characteristics. As an intuitionist, Ross asserted that the right- and wrong-making characteristics of actions were rationally self-evident in the same way that truths in mathematics are self-evident.[4] Just as we come to learn that two plus two does not equal three, we come to see that lying, whatever the circumstance, is an unfitting characteristic of the way in which we are relating ourselves to others, and we come to call that unfitting interpersonal relationship morally wrong. Once we, as a community or civilization, have come to see this over time, the wrong-making character of lying is self-evident to us.

Intuitionists, then, are characterized by the following metaethical claims:

1) that ethical assertions are cognitive and can be judged as true or false;
2) that ethical terms refer to unique or simple non-natural characteristics of reality;
3) that ethical assertions are not descriptive of, and cannot be identified with, any particular empirical characteristic of reality.

NONCOGNITIVISM

There is another group of moral philosophers who agree with Moore and other intuitionists that moral assertions are not descriptions of empirical characteristics of reality. But this same group of philosophers took sharp issue with the intuitionists on two important points: they denied that moral assertions refer to rationally intuited, non-natural characteristics of reality, and they denied that it is possible to judge whether moral assertions are true or false. These philosophers limited judgments of what is true or false to statements that are verifiable by reference to empirical facts known only through our senses and to statements that are logically correct or incorrect. Moral assertions were considered to be neither empirical assertions nor true or false by definition as in logic and mathematics.

One of the more significant noncognitivist theories is emotivism. The twentieth-century moral philosopher C. L. Stevenson stated it in one of its more influential forms.[5] Stevenson claimed that moral statements are primarily persuasive in function. They evince or express a certain kind of emotional attitude. The influence of G. E. Moore is clearly evident in the following passage where Stevenson is rejecting all attempts to consider moral assertions as scientifically knowable:

> No matter what set of scientifically knowable properties a thing may have (says Moore, in effect), you will find, on careful introspection, that it is an open question to ask whether anything having these properties is *good*. It is difficult to believe that this recurrent question is a totally confused one or that it seems open only because of the ambiguity of "good." Rather, we must be using some sense of "good" which is not definable, relevantly, in terms of anything scientifically knowable. That is, the scientific method is not sufficient for ethics.[6]

Stevenson described the meaning of an ethical term like *good* as follows: "X is good means I approve of X; do so as well."[7] In offering this understanding of *good*, Stevenson is not claiming that *good* is identical with a particular attitude of approval, but rather that claims made on behalf of *good* imply a favorable attitude toward X that encompasses a unique desire that this favorable attitude be shared by others. Moral utterances, therefore, have this unique quality long noted within ethics of expecting that what is favored as good will be universally so favored.

Accepting a view like Stevenson's has very serious implications for how we view the possibility of justifying moral judgments. If, like Stevenson, we think of moral assertions as assertions expressing our own favorable or unfavorable attitudes which we hope will be shared, moral discourse is then largely relegated to the area of private opinion. Stevenson was very aware of this grave implication and sought to show the extent to which discussions and reflections upon moral judgments did relate to matters of fact. But since Stevenson could see no logical connection between any particular set of facts and any particular moral judgment, moral rhetoric, in the end, is seen as a form of persuasion, primarily emotional and nonscientific rather than rational and scientific in character. It is not surprising that Stevenson and others sharing his point of view did not see normative ethics as a part of the science of ethics at all. Only metaethics, the attempt to characterize the nature of moral discourse, constitutes, for them, the formal discipline of ethics. Normative ethics is the concern of politicians and preachers and is not a part of ethics as a field of knowledge.

Many contemporary noncognitivists have parted company with the emotivists. It is very generally acknowledged now among ethicists that moral assertions are not simply expressions of our favorable or unfavorable attitudes and our desire to have others share them. Indeed, they are not primarily expressions of our emotions at all. Furthermore, it has been noted that if one takes seriously, as Stevenson does, Moore's open-question test, then Stevenson's own theory can be defeated by it. Of any X concerning which I might say, ''I approve of X, I expect you to do so as well,'' one can sensibly and logically ask whether what I approve and wish you to approve is good.

Frankena has expressed dissatisfaction with noncognitivist theories generally, asserting rather emphatically that ''an ethical judgment claims that it will stand up under scrutiny by oneself and others in the light of the most careful thinking and the best knowledge, and that rival judgments will not stand up under such scrutiny.''[8] In the end, it seems to Frankena that previous noncognitivist theories, like ethical relativism, allow or even insist that conflicting basic judgments, whether between individuals or between cultures, may be justified or justifiable. Sharing the view we have expressed above that ethical relativism has not been proved, he tries to forge an ethical theory that is very akin to naturalism, but without accepting the notion that moral statements are empirically or in any other sense verifiable.

Very briefly, Frankena holds that we can justify or offer reasons for our moral judgments if we adopt what he calls the "moral point of view." He describes this view in the following way:

> One is taking the moral point of view if and only if (a) one is making normative judgments about actions, desires, dispositions, intentions, motives, persons, or traits of character; (b) one is willing to universalize one's judgments; (c) one's reasons for one's judgments consist of facts about what the things judged do to the lives of sentient beings in terms of promoting or distributing nonmoral good and evil; and (d) when the judgment is about oneself or one's own actions, one's reasons include such facts about what one's own actions and dispositions do to the lives of other sentient beings as such, if others are affected. One has a morality or moral action-guide only if and insofar as one makes normative judgments from this point of view and is guided by them.[9]

Frankena's account of how we are able to give reasons for our moral judgments and why it is that it makes sense to carry on a debate about what is morally right or wrong is an attractive one. However, as we shall now endeavor to show, there is still a problem remaining with such a theory, and it is for a resolution of that problem that we now turn to consider what has been called the ideal observer theory.

NATURALISM: THE IDEAL OBSERVER THEORY

Contemporary naturalist metaethical theories attempt to learn from the insights of the various theories we have already described but do not find any of them completely satisfactory. Naturalism shares with noncognitivist theories a rejection of the claim that ethical terms refer to nonnatural or nonempirical characteristics known by intuition. In opposition to the noncognitivists, however, naturalists take the view that moral statements do admit of truth and falsity and are in some sense empirically verifiable. Naturalism takes its name from this affirmation of the empirically verifiable nature of moral judgments.[10] How is it that naturalists are led to assert these propositions?

The most serious problem for intuitionism is that it cannot

adequately deal with the problem of errors in intuiting. If, as intuitionists believe, it is possible to identify certain right- or wrong-making characteristics of actions and to say of them that they express something true known to reason, then how will we discover which person or group is in error when two persons or groups disagree as to whether a particular characteristic of an action is right-making? To try to deal with this question, A. C. Ewing, a prominent intuitionist among moral philosophers, lists the following four conditions that facilitate errors:

1) lack of experience;
2) lack of sufficient attention to the facts;
3) intellectual confusion; and
4) mental abnormality.[11]

On the face of it, this would seem to be a helpful list, but it does not solve the problem of error. If one accepts a list like this, then one must affirm a proposition to the effect that "people of such and such kind are more likely to intuit correctly than. . . ." But why should this proposition be accepted? If you answer on grounds of intuition, then you are involved in an infinite regress.[12] This is not to reject Ewing's understanding of certain conditions that facilitate error, but rather to indicate that the reasons for the cogency of these conditions need to be grounded in something other than intuition.

As indicated above, Frankena, like Ewing, has given us a plausible account of some of the conditions under which errors or differences in our moral judgments might be corrected or rendered more rational. But again, as in Ewing's theory, one is left without a reason for adopting a proposition to the effect that "someone adopting the moral point of view will make a more rationally justifiable moral judgment than. . . ." Presumably the same kind of infinite regress is involved, i.e., in order to claim that some moral assertion is more rational than another because it is made from the moral point of view, one would first have to adopt the moral point of view.

Naturalists share with Frankena the strong conviction that moral judgments have an objective quality in the sense that some of our moral claims can be seen as part of what we know to be true about the real world, while other moral judgments turn out on examination to be false, or at least not demonstrably part of what we know. The foundation of this conviction that moral assertions admit of truth or falsity has been sought in examining the way in which and the extent to which moral assertions are empirically verifiable.

Naturalists have not ignored the insights of Moore. Contemporary naturalists would not attempt to make some simple identification of a moral term like *right* with some specific empirical quality of the world such as our desires, pleasures, motives, or the like. Nor do naturalists fall into the error of claiming that right or good can simply be identified with some existing natural law or pattern. Of anything that exists in nature, we can ask whether it is right or wrong to destroy, change or preserve it. And the same question can be asked of any existing pattern of material, animal, or human behavior. Even if from some religious perspective we take the view that everything that is, is in some sense good, we would still be left with deciding when and how certain things will be destroyed, changed, or preserved, and on what grounds we will behave one way rather than another toward our fellow human beings, animals, and the rest of our environment.

The most plausible naturalist theory is one that incorporates a number of the suggestions being made in theories like those of Ewing and Frankena, and for that matter, incorporates elements that have been found in almost all moral reflection and practice. We refer here to the ideal observer theory as it has been recently stated by Roderick Firth.[13] Firth defines the statement "X is right" as "X would be approved by an ideal observer who is omniscient, omnipercipient, disinterested, dispassionate, and otherwise normal." Here Firth is taking the view that knowledge that is mediated by our perceptions of reality is something that we obtain under certain kinds of conditions. Stating the conditions under which we obtain particular perceptions will define what we mean by a particular word that we use to identify some part of the real world.

In the moral sphere, there are certain conditions, as Ewing, Frankena, and others have noted, under which we can confirm or deny our own or someone else's perception of something as right or wrong, good or evil. These conditions can be stated as characteristics of some hypothetical being who, if possessed of those characteristics, would be able to make a correct moral judgment. As in any quest to obtain corroborating evidence of a scientific hypothesis, theory, or observation, the quest for truth in the area of morality yields clues as to how we go about verifying our claims by providing an analysis of what it is we are trying to verify. We come to understand what we mean by terms like *right* when we come to identify the processes by which we would try to convince ourselves or others that what we say is right is in fact right. Let us look now at some of these conditions or characteristics of an ideal observer specified by Firth's definition of what is right.

First of all, there is omniscience. It is surely clear in all our discussions and reflections on moral judgments that we are not ready to accept ill-informed judgments as true. Many people were reluctant, for example, to take the view that U.S. involvement in South Vietnam was immoral until they had much more knowledge about the actual situation in South Vietnam than was obtainable in the early phases of that war. Turning to the area of medicine, it is very clear why it is that we are concerned about informed consent on the part of patients. If patients do not know the nature of their illness and the nature of the kinds of interventions available for dealing with such an illness, they can in no way make a moral choice. How can we say that the patient who is uninformed has any basis for claiming to have done the right or the wrong thing by submitting or failing to submit to a particular medical intervention? It is clearly recognized that people are to be held morally responsible for what they know and cannot be expected to do what is morally right and correct unless they have the knowledge needed to make a particular decision. No one would consider a court that failed to investigate the facts of a case, or failed to do so conscientiously and thoroughly, as a place in which justice can be done. What Firth's theory says is that ideally to know what is right would, among other things, involve knowing everything. Indeed, some of the uncertainty and ambiguities that surround some of our moral judgments stem from the fact that we are not able to have all of the information that we ideally need to make these judgments, but we can improve them by improving the amount and quality of our information.

What does Firth mean by omnipercipience? This refers to an ability to place ourselves in the position of those who are affected by our actions. If we are to make a correct moral judgment, it will be necessary vividly to imagine how we and others will be affected by the particular action or policy being contemplated. Medical professionals are very aware of this important ingredient in moral decision-making. Sometimes this point is overstated when health professionals claim that only those who are confronted by the ill and suffering persons about whom decisions are being made are in a position to make a proper or correct moral judgment about what is to be done for them. Nevertheless, it is difficult when we are not in the presence of suffering persons to act with their needs or welfare in mind. For example, very few if any persons possessed of ample food at their tables would turn away a starving child seated at that table and refuse to give that child food. Yet at the same time, it is easy to forget one's resolve to give something to CARE or OXFAM or Church World Service this year again to help some such starving child in another country. Those who opposed the war in Vietnam knew very well what effect it would have to show pictures in the United States of napalmed South Vietnamese children. It would certainly stimulate our imagination of the ill effects of the particular way in which the United States was conducting war in South Vietnam. Similarly on the other side of this equation, it was possible for members of the Nazi party to insulate themselves from imagining how some of their own orders would affect people. Had they failed to insulate themselves from imagining what was happening as a result of ordering others to forced labor or the gas chambers, they would very likely have found their role in the Nazi party totally intolerable.

Disinterestedness and dispassionateness are qualities that are widely recognized and often referred to as impartiality. To be disinterested and dispassionate is not to be devoid of interests and passions. Disinterestedness and dispassionateness can be described in a rough and rather practical way as forms of taking into account various interests and passions.[14] Thus, for example, we cannot expect a disinterested judgment in a court if we do not have some procedure by which the interests of both the party being accused and the party making the accusations are able to present the facts that are in their respective interests to put before the court. We insist, therefore, on a mechanism that will defend the interests of all parties to a dispute. We do this by pitting against one another lawyers who seek conscientiously to defend the interests of their clients and we consider it unfair for one party in a dispute not to have such loyal and conscientious representation. We have found also that the influence of interests and passions can be very subtle, so that our confidence that justice will be done in a jury trial is increased, for example, if in trying a black we do not countenance an all-white jury. Indeed, potential jurors are screened in a variety of ways in an attempt to weed out ascertainable prejudices against the person on trial.

It is noteworthy that the whole American governmental system seeks to attain some approximation of disinterestedness and dispassionateness by a separation of legislative, administrative, and judicial powers. No one would claim perfection of this system, but the point of it is clearly to make it more difficult for decisions to be made from the point of view of particular vested interests or loyalties. It is commonly recognized that power is corrupting, and one important condition under which this occurs is that there is no procedure or competing group that mounts effective opposition to the. interests of the person in power.

There are some less lofty examples of how our institutions implicitly recognize the importance of disinterestedness and dispassionateness. We would not, for instance, permit judges to try their own children nor do we expect physicians to perform surgery on their own family members. There is wide recognition in the medical profession that ways to implement disinterestedness and dispassionateness are extremely important. A case in point is the insistence that a physician who makes a judgment as to whether brain-death criteria are met for a particular patient whose organs are sought for transplantation should not be a member of the transplant team seeking an organ from that patient. Examples of this kind are easily multiplied.

When Firth adds to the requisite qualities of an ideal observer already discussed the further stipulation that an ideal observer would be otherwise normal, he does not wish, for understandable reasons, to indulge in any strict definition of normality. Rather, he is seeking to leave vague and open other qualities of an ideal moral judge that may or may not be relevant and to call attention to the fact that there may be serious deficiencies, say, of intellect or emotion, that if an ideal observer had them would adversely affect the other necessary qualities for making a correct moral judgment. Firth recognizes that all this is quite vague, but it is purposely so. It is undoubtedly the case that we have difficulty in obtaining agreement with respect to our moral judgments, because we also have difficulty in discovering all the conditions under which, in principle, agreement would be possible.

We should not think that in proposing an ideal observer theory Firth is claiming that people who are trying to rectify a disagreement or justify a particular moral judgment are necessarily aware of being or trying to be something like an ideal observer. Rather, what Firth is trying to do is describe the procedures that individuals and societies use, or would on reflection use, when they do try to correct their own or other people's moral judgments, and he finds that these can be conveniently stated as ideal properties of a hypothetical being. It should be evident that no human being has the qualities of an ideal observer, and it should be no less evident that persons and institutions do concern themselves with trying to realize or approximate the conditions that are specified by the characteristics of an ideal observer.

The ideal observer theory is not new. There are references to impartial spectators and analogues to ideal observers in a great deal of the literature of moral philosophy. We can see also that religious conceptions of God can be seen as at least in part endeavoring to describe what an ideal moral judge and agent would be like. Firth is aware that his own particular description of an ideal observer is not exactly what you would get in other traditions and cultures. Nor does he argue that his particular theory is complete or in every detail correct, but he does see it as an appropriate description of the logic of moral discourse for which there is evidence in the experience of individuals and societies by no means confined to Western experience. Institutional and individual attempts to achieve some kind of impartial judgment are well known to all of us, particularly in the context of trying to settle disputes among individuals and groups.

Certainly within moral philosophy and religious ethics, we see a great deal of convergence around Firth's notion of the characteristics of an ideal moral judge. The distinctive contribution of Firth's particular version of the ideal observer theory is that he has stated it not only with great clarity but also in a form in which it escapes certain objections that have been made to empiricist theories. For example, Firth's theory cannot be rejected simply by an appeal to the "open question test." It is not at all self-evident that it makes sense to question whether X is right when X has been judged to be so under the conditions that define an ideal observer. What Firth has done is base his view of the meaning of ethical terms on an analysis of how these terms function in actual moral discourse. Those who disagree with Firth's definition of ethical terms like *right* can simply be invited to examine how they seek to determine what is right and to reflect on the way in which our institutions are designed and redesigned to facilitate fact-finding, sensitivity, and some form of impartiality in seeking ways of handling and resolving conflict regarding what is right or just. Indeed, as we indicated earlier, the governmental system itself is at least on the face of it designed to accomplish this kind of corrective process in the formulation and implementation of policy.

Some readers will recognize, then, that Firth's formulation of an ideal observer theory is a rather pragmatic one that can be defined, redefined, and refined. In use it provides some simple, workable criteria for checking out our judgments, grounded both in logic and experience. It invites dialogue and participation in the structures of our societies on the part of diverse individuals and groups. It warns against situations for which there are no procedural and structural safeguards against vested interests, particular passions, impoverished imagination, and ignorance about factual and situational realities.

In order to help the reader picture how it is that the ideal observer theory may and does enter into the formulation and reformulation of moral judgments and policies, let us briefly examine two illustrative applications of its criteria. The first example is drawn from existing practices and policies that guide decisions regarding the use of humans in medical research. The second example is a partial suggestion as to what would be implied by systematically using the ideal observer theory in trying to decide what kinds of population policies would be most rational and most morally justifiable.

Practices associated with scientific research in medicine provide a partial demonstration of how social forces may move in the direction of increasingly realizing ideal observer criteria to guide social policy and individual decisions. Within the medical profession itself, it has been increasingly realized that a physician interested in doing a scientific study would sometimes be involved in a serious conflict of interest where the subjects for such a study are also patients of that same physician. This certainly occurs where the scientific research in question is not of any therapeutic benefit to those who are asked to take part in it. In such situations, the medical profession has seen the importance of providing assurance that patients will be cared for and their interests looked after by physicians who do not have any direct or immediate interest in any research project for which these patients are being sought as subjects. Needless to say, this is one way to help bring about a certain measure of impartiality (disinterestedness and dispassionateness) and to secure for patients a better knowledge of the true risks or benefits of any particular experiment in which they are asked to participate.

The American Government has taken the view that it is responsible for seeing to it that scientific investigations funded by its agencies, such as the National Institute of Health (NIH), do not violate the rights of research subjects. Hence, regulations have evolved that include a requirement of informed consent as well as assessments of the risks and benefits of any experiment to assure that risks are minimized and that benefits outweigh risks.[15] To enforce these regulations, the NIH requires institutions doing research to set up committees that include people trained in the sciences in which the research is taking place, but which include also non-scientists, particularly people with some expertise in ethics and law. These committees check research protocols to see if risks and benefits have been properly assessed by the investigators and informed consent clearly and reasonably provided for.

These NIH regulations seem precisely designed to more nearly realize impartiality, a vivid imagination as to how people are affected by given experiments, and a process of both increasing knowledge about actual and potential risks and benefits and increasing the extent to which subjects share that knowledge. NIH has implicitly, if not explicitly recognized that those engaged in research have a vested interest in carrying out that research and in obtaining money for it. Therefore, these committees have been set up to try to compensate for any biases investigators may have that would make them underestimate risks, overestimate benefits, and be overzealous in recruiting subjects. Needless to say, what NIH is doing is a very rough-hewn process and there is no attempt on my part to claim that this set of arrangements is ideal in theory or practice. All that I am arguing here is that it is a method for more nearly approximating ideal conditions for undertaking research in a way that will not violate the most basic rights of human beings to life, liberty, and the just pursuit of their own happiness.

In chapter 2 we described and analyzed the major population policy alternatives currently under debate. For the purposes of this analysis, we drew on descriptive categories devised by Ralph B. Potter in one of his previous studies of a policy debate.[16] These categories describe major variables, sometimes explicit, sometimes implicit, in terms of which reasons for agreement and disagreement on policy can be ascertained. As we shall now see, analyzing policy debates with the use of Potter's descriptive categories yields a great deal of the information we need to discover the degree to which a given policy position has satisfied the criteria for rationally determining what is right, namely, knowing all the facts, vividly imagining how others are affected by the policy in question, and achieving disinterestedness and dispassionateness, i.e., impartiality.

With respect to knowing all the facts, Potter's categories alert us to two types of facts and factual assumptions. There are facts and assumptions that are made within the context of the various natural and social sciences. There are other facts and factual assumptions about the real world regarding which observations and systematic reflection may be done, but the substantiation of these depend upon social experiments on a vast scale that are both difficult to initiate as well as to assess with any kind of finality. In this connection, Potter used the expression theological or quasi-theological assumptions about reality.

As we look at suggested population policies from the point of view of knowing all the facts, it is apparent that some of the information that is needed for making rational decisions about the correct and morally right policy will be difficult to obtain for at least two reasons. First of all, those who would devise population policy need to know a great deal more about the kinds of benefits people derive from having children, and in turn, why it is that these benefits are sometimes tied to small and sometimes to large families. These data are difficult to obtain. This brings us to our second point, namely, that some of the knowledge, including the knowledge just cited, will probably only be obtainable if we are able to initiate social experiments in which the conditions thought to be conducive to low birth rates are introduced in such a way that they may be compared with conditions that have been associated with high birth rates. As we indicated in chapter 2, the initiation of such social experiments will hinge in large part on whether it is possible to argue that the social experiments being introduced are both just and beneficial. These, as we indicated in chapter 2, are explicitly moral considerations. It is important, therefore, to examine and develop explicitly one's modes of moral reasoning. We shall return to this point shortly.

Potter's categories also ask us to look at the loyalties both of those who propose and those who are affected by our moral decisions or policies. In the political arena, it is especially difficult to achieve impartiality on the part of any single individual or group making decisions. Hence, to best achieve some approximation of impartiality in formulating, implementing, and achieving acceptance for population policies, it is necessary to have input, through various forms of representation and participation, from all groups that will be affected by those policies. It is not enough simply to represent majority interests in any region or society where the interests of minorities are significantly diverse from those of any majority or other powerful political group in a position to ignore the wishes of such minorities. Impartiality in the political sphere, therefore, requires a high degree of representative and participatory democracy, so that those communities for which policies are conceptualized and actualized do not fall victim to false claims on the part of a power elite. It is notorious how often a policy defended as beneficial for all is, in fact, mainly, if not entirely, beneficial to the group seeking to bring about that policy.

In seeking to stimulate a vivid imagination of how people are affected by a given population policy and also to achieve some degree of impartiality, it is important to gather information about the needs, interests, aspirations, and values of the persons concerned. But in order to do so, attention must be given to the methods used. In its investigations, the population field has put an undue reliance on materials and questions devised by people of cultures in many ways alien, or certainly different from the cultures being studied. Whatever the merit of the questionnaires and structured interviews being used, they often fail to discover what is most salient to those being investigated. It may certainly be argued that various forms of participant observation, as well as direct involvement in the planning and implementation of a given population policy by some of the very people implicated, would enhance the possibility of achieving the kind of informed imagination and impartiality which is required for rational policy decisions.

Given the complexity and incompleteness of the knowledge needed for justifying population policies, the social experiments that would test conflicting views will largely be accepted or rejected on the basis of our moral reasoning. Although there are a number of moral considerations associated with decisions about how to choose among alternative population policies, for illustrative purposes I chose in chapter 2 to focus on justice because, among other reasons, it has become a central concept for those debating alternative population policies. One reason for this is that population policies tend to have a differential effect on various couples and groups within the society for which the policy is designed. This point we amply illustrated in chapter 2. What we wish to indicate briefly now is the way in which the ideal observer criteria have influenced the conception of justice that was used and advocated in that chapter.

In chapter 2 we rejected a conception of justice that would either fail to benefit or further disadvantage those who are already the least advantaged members of a given society. Certain utilitarian conceptions of justice employ a standard, namely the greatest good for the greatest number, that would allow us to consider a policy as just if that policy would secure the most beneficial effects on the whole, even though it might mean that some individuals or groups would not share in these benefits and may even be further disadvantaged by the policy in question. It is difficult to see how justice on this view would satisfy a requirement for impartiality, where the interests and needs of everyone in a society would receive due recognition. And if, also, a policy is to be based on a vivid imagination of how various parties are affected, it would be impossible to tolerate a policy that would disadvantage the already disadvantaged.

In chapter 2 we introduced Rawls's conception of justice as the one most likely to provide a satisfactory way of evaluating the justness of population policy.[17] This was by no means an arbitrary choice. Rawls argued for the rationality of conceiving justice in a way that implicitly, at least, recognized the force of the ideal observer criteria. He had people imagine that they were in a hypothetical situation in which they had the opportunity to choose the society in which they would live and the principles by means of which the positions in that society would be ordered. Built into this hypothetical situation is an assumption of self-interest, mutual disinterestedness, and ignorance as to what position they would have in the society they were choosing and ordering.

Using this device, Rawls has assumed that the rationality of principles of justice require impartiality as well as a lively imagination of how all persons, including oneself, are affected by various social policies. Rawls came to the conclusion that people would not trade off their most basic rights, so that one principle they would affirm would be that of maximizing liberty to the extent compatible with like liberty for all. But he also inferred that persons under ideal observer conditions would accept certain differences and policies with differential effects. The principle on which they would do so would be one in which differences would be mutually advantageous, that is, advantageous to the society as a whole and to each of its members, with particular attentiveness to those members of the society who may in any way be disadvantaged relative to others. Self-interested individuals who are ignorant of how a policy will affect them and who are aware that they might be subject to any of the possible differential effects of that policy will be stimulated to take every person's interest into account and will certainly have a lively imagination of how everyone is affected, since in principle, their self-interest requires them to do so.

Very briefly, then, we have sketched the relationship between the criteria for rationality generated by the ideal observer theory and a specific conception of justice, in this case, that of John Rawls. In doing so, we have tried to give readers some indication as to why it is that Rawls's particular conception of justice was featured in our discussion of population policy in chapter 2, namely because it seems best to satisfy these criteria. This by no means settles the question as to what is the best way of thinking about justice or whether Rawls's discussion of it is as complete and as refined as would be rationally ideal. Our only claim would be that refinements of his and other conceptions of justice would, if they conscientiously seek to approximate the truth, make use of the kinds of considerations rendered specific by articulating and working with the characteristics of an ideal observer. As we shall see in the final chapter that follows, there is no deductive relationship between the characteristics of an ideal observer and the moral principles that such an ideal observer would select and identify as such.[18] No, what we have here, as we shall see in that chapter, is a rough and pragmatic process of trying to discern what is true and false, something we try to do not only with respect to particular acts, but also with respect to our views of what will count as moral principles.

What we have been suggesting about the moral assessment of population policy in this chapter is that categories of the type developed by Ralph Potter will help to elicit the kind of data and analysis to which one can then apply the criteria of the ideal observer theory in order to try to make a reasonable decision about what population policy is most morally justifiable. It is important to note that although Firth's ideal observer theory claims to specify certain ideal conditions (what we are here calling criteria of rationality) on the basis of which ethical statements can be characterized as true or false, this carries with it no connotation of dogmatism or of claims to certitude. The theory recognizes that moral assertions still carry with them a great deal of ambiguity. But they are not seen as totally or systematically ambiguous, for they do admit of definite intellectual, social, and political, corrective processes, however imprecise these may be. Indeed, if we believe that ideally the truth in matters of moral judgment depends on omniscience, omnipercipience, and some kind of complete impartiality, we immediately recognize that no single human being or even the best court in the land is able to achieve these ideal conditions. Individuals and institutions, therefore, will be variable in their moral judgments.

We should not, however, minimize the advantages of Firth's theory. It is one that indicates how moral judgments are and can be empirically verifiable, prompting us to locate sources of disagreement and of potential and actual error by seeking more facts and by improving our imagination and our impartiality. This does not mean that we should always expect to achieve complete, or on some difficult matters, widespread agreement as to what is morally right or wrong, good or evil. It means, rather, that we have methods for trying to work out policies that do not require resort to violence or a break in our relationships toward those individuals or groups with whom we find ourselves in disagreement. There is from the standpoint of Firth's theory some ground for a continuing dialogue and peaceful compromise among persons and groups who disagree with one another on vital moral issues. Clearly Firth's ideal observer theory is totally compatible with the affirmation of tolerance in the various senses in which we have used that term in previous chapters. Indeed, it provides an explicit rationale for tolerance and a basis for healing those divisions among people which put a strain upon our mutual tolerance.

We turn now to our final chapter to discuss further the way in which the normative enterprise of identifying and understanding moral principles is related to the endeavor to increase the degree to which our choices of moral principles are rendered more reasonable. Such a discussion would not be complete without some indication as to how and to what extent it is possible to make choices in situations where moral principles conflict. We will therefore take up some practical instances to illustrate how moral principles themselves, and certain kinds of reasoning about them, can provide modest but important help in resolving serious moral dilemmas. The chapter will conclude with a brief analysis of the relation between religion and morality.

Chapter VII—Suggestions for Further Reading

Readers will find fairly systematic discussions of metaethics in the works on moral philosophy mentioned in the notes for this chapter as well as the suggested readings at the end of chapter 1. Chapters 7–9 in Richard B. Brandt, *Ethical Theory* (Englewood Cliffs, N.J.: Prentice-Hall, 1959), are among the best assessments of metaethical options within contemporary moral philosophy.

chapter viii
the moral life

We are living in a period of history when all of us are carefully taught that scientific facts and truths can only be discovered with the use of rigorous methods developed and refined within the sciences. Without such methods, the gains of science will not be sustained or augmented for future generations. With great diligence, scientists teach and refine their methods. But so committed are scientists to the efficacy of their methods and the truth of their discoveries that the late Jacob Bronowski, himself an eminent and well-known scientist, has observed that science and its methodology would, if lost, be reinvented.[1]

Scientists, however, are not asking us to reinvent scientific methodology. They are fully aware that centuries of thought and investigation are behind the scientific community's present ability to extend knowledge. Nevertheless, as we noted above, Bronowski is convinced that human beings could reinvent the powerful tools of science. There is something terribly ironic, then, in Bronowski's claim that certain values characterizing human dignity, science, and scientists are utterly new. Unwittingly, or so it seems, Bronowski and his fellow scientists are prepared to reinvent the Mosaic covenant. Now everything that we have argued for in this book would say that human beings can indeed reinvent the Mosaic covenant, but like scientists in other fields, ethicists would hope that the gains of several centuries of thought and investigation would be cultivated by each generation and passed on to the next, just as they are in other sciences.

What, you may ask, does it mean to say that Bronowski and his fellow scientists appear ready to reinvent the Mosaic covenant? Let us examine some examples cited by Bronowski.

> If I steal money from any person, there may be no harm done by the mere transfer of possession; he may not feel the loss, or it may even prevent him from using the money badly. But I cannot help doing this great wrong towards Man, that I make myself dishonest. What hurts society is not that it should lose its property, but that it should become a den of thieves; for then it must cease to be society.[2]

Here a scientist is affirming the injunction not to steal for the same reason that this prohibition found its place in the Mosaic covenant originally, namely to make community possible. A similar point is made about the necessity for testing our beliefs and the recognition that the foundations of our social life depend on trust and trustworthiness, both in the sense that we do not lie to ourselves or others and in the sense that we do not justify beliefs for which we have insufficient evidence:

> In like manner, if I let myself believe anything on insufficient evidence, there may be no great harm done by the mere belief; it may be true after all, or I may never have occasion to exhibit it in outward acts. But I cannot help doing this great wrong towards Man, that I make myself credulous. The danger to society is not merely that it should believe wrong things, though that is great enough; but that it should become credulous.[3]

Bronowski is no less emphatic than the Mosaic covenant in rejecting "false witness" in the quest for truth:

> The test of truth is the known factual evidence, and no glib expediency nor reason of state can justify the smallest self-deception in that. Our work is of a piece, in the large and in detail; so that if we silence one scruple about our means, we infect ourselves and our ends together.[4]

From the standpoint of ethics, it is somewhat surprising that Bronowski, with all his learning, views his stout defense of moral prohibitions against stealing and lying as something new and as a unique contribution of the scientific community. Of course, as an ethicist, I am not surprised to find these endorsements of the moral life "reinvented," as it were, by the scientific community. This is precisely what one would expect from a conscientious effort to seek truth and form community. But just as the scientific community strives mightily to keep its methods in good repair and ever alert to new discoveries, ethics also strives to do the same. Ethics, however, currently labors under a tremendous handicap. Every schoolchild is introduced to science and its methods. The same is no longer predictably true with respect to ethics.

At this point one of the peculiar problems of ethics clearly emerges. Many of us, including myself, do not have to make daily decisions about the truth or falsity of particular scientific theories and findings. All of us, however, do have to make moral judgments on a daily basis. On the one hand, this means that all of us gain some expertise and experience in ethics. On the other hand, this means that we are less than well prepared for life if we have had no exposure to the formal discipline of ethical thought.

What we are saying here should not be quickly dismissed as a plea for ethics in our educational curricula. Important as a debate about that may be, we do not wish to initiate that discussion here. No, our point lies elsewhere. We are simply claiming that it is important for a society to have as much awareness of the efficacy of ethical methods as it does of the efficacy of various other scientific methodologies. And if such awareness is lost, the substance and methods of ethics *will* have to be reinvented. In this last chapter we want to say a little bit more about why this is so, and why the substance and methods of ethics are so important and so predictably a part of human life.

MORAL PRINCIPLES AND ETHICAL PROCEDURES

In the previous chapter, we argued that the ideal observer theory provides one of the most plausible descriptions of how we would go about justifying our moral judgments. Our moral judgments do not only assert what we believe or think about the rightness or wrongness of actions and institutions and the goodness or badness of persons. We also make judgments regarding the moral principles to which we appeal when deciding what is right or wrong, good or bad. What, then, is the connection between moral principles and the ideal conditions specified by the ideal observer theory?

What we would claim is that a set of moral principles enunciated by W. D. Ross, along with the amendments suggested in chapters 4 and 5, constitute what would be experienced as moral principles by a hypothetical being having the characteristics of an ideal observer.[5] Clearly there is no easy way of testing this claim other than to ask people to reflect upon and argue about whether they also would affirm certain right- and wrong-making characteristics of actions as moral principles. The recognition both of what conditions are ideal for making the most nearly correct moral judgments, and of what relationships, personal and institutional, are morally significant arises out of a process of individual and social dialogue, institutional testing, and intellec-

The Moral Life

tual reflection. Although this is a dynamic, on-going, historical process, it does not repudiate the fact that we do seem to be able to perceive some human relationships that have the constancy of moral principles as identified in chapters 3, 4, and 5. The chart on the following page allows the reader to examine these moral principles and obtain specific references to where in the book they are analyzed.

As readers will recall, Ross took the view that what we identify and promulgate as moral principles is self-evidently known. Now we have agreed with those who consider any appeal to self-evident intuitions as an insufficient ground for affirming what is true or false about our moral judgments. Nevertheless, Ross is making a point that should not be lost, however inadequate intuitionism is as a theory of moral justification.

Both rule utilitarians and formalists are agreed that a great many of our moral decisions are most immediately justified by appeals to moral principles. This means that the degree to which individuals and groups in a given society actually behave in accord with moral principles will depend in large part on how self-evident it is for them to do so. By *self-evident* here I mean that they do so automatically where no reflection occurs, and they do not question acting on these particular moral principles when there is time for reflection. This is no new observation we are making. Aristotle took the view that a society should habituate its young to act morally; only much later in their mature years would it be possible for them to recognize the reasons for behaving in certain ways rather than others, for being moral rather than immoral. If such a process of education and development is to take place within any given society, that society will have to have a lively sense of what moral principles carry with them a high enough degree of certitude and moral weightiness to be instilled, exemplified, and dramatized by its customs and institutions, particularly its educational and socializing institutions.

The nurturance of the moral life of a community depends, then, on a vivid sense of what it takes to be an ideal moral judge, and of the moral principles that have been and are to be gleaned by the reflection of an ideal moral judge upon the moral significance of our interpersonal and interinstitutional relationships. Some would say that the teaching of moral principles and of how reasonably to justify them is a matter for individual families and for religious

TABLE OF MORAL PRINCIPLES

Human Relations on Which Perceived Obligations Identified as Moral Principles Are Based	Moral Principles (defined on pp. 52–54; 98–100)
Previous acts of the agent(s) involving fidelity	Promise-keeping (see. p. 63) Truth-telling (see p. 63)
Previous wrongful acts	Reparation (see p. 63)
Previous beneficial actions of others	Gratitude (see p. 63) Most stringent form of this obligation is gratitude to those who give and sustain life (see pp. 93–94)
Distribution of rights, benefits, and injuries	Justice (see pp. 103-5)
Benefiting others	Beneficence (see pp. 105–13) Doing good (see pp. 105–10; 112–13) Removing evil (see pp. 112–13) Preventing evil (see pp. 112–13)
Not injuring ourselves and others	Non-maleficence (refraining from evil) (see pp. 92–105; 111–12) Most stringent forms of evil, because most destructive of institutions requisite to community, are: Stealing (see pp. 94–96; 99) Killing (see pp. 94; 99–105) Bearing false witness (see pp. 96–98) Infidelity in a marital convenant (see p. 96)
Improving ourselves	Being morally virtuous (see pp. 110–13) Moral conscientiousness (see pp. 110–11) Moral perceptivity (see p. 111) (These moral virtues are best realized in emulating and striving to be like the ideal moral judge.)

institutions to carry on if they so choose. To be sure, one would hope that families and religious organizations would teach, demonstrate, and symbolize the moral life in all of its aspects. However, to the extent that families and religious organizations derive intellectual sustenance from educational institutions and scholarly enterprises celebrated in those institutions, they may find themselves increasingly skeptical of past insights, that once seemed self-evident, in an intellectual climate where no rational defense of these past insights is usually offered and where appeals to self-evidence are understandably greeted with skepticism. Equally understandable, however, in this situation is the increasing recognition in some quarters of the importance of rediscovering and refurbishing the humanistic disciplines which have provided much of the substance of our moral life, and which through philosophical and theological investigations have continued to refine our reasoning about right and wrong.

Let us summarize now the importance of identifying and articulating moral principles that will serve as guidelines for moral decision-making. Moral principles, when specifically and clearly identified as such, provide the following advantages:

1) They emphasize the multiplicity of moral claims that come to us in almost every situation. The moral complexity of our actions and policies is thereby made explicit.

2) They offer substance to teach the young as well as to inform daily policy-making.

3) They provide a way of drawing upon past wisdom. Only if we know what has already previously been identified as morally significant do we recognize where genuine innovation in our moral perceptions is or should be taking place.

4) They help us to identify unique moral claims. Where our moral principles are clearly articulated, and only where they are, do we discover what appear to be unique moral elements in particular cases or situations, unique in the sense that they go beyond the moral claims recognized in our moral principles and lead us to add to or change those principles.

Principles may help us, but, readers may ask, what guidance, if any, do they provide when they are in conflict with one another? And conflicts may also arise, readers may rightly point out, when it is not possible to satisfy at the same time the moral claims upon us of two different individuals or groups. Of course, in chapter 5 we did try to indicate that certain moral principles have more weight than others. Although this is of some help in guiding us with respect to conflicts among principles, and theoretically every moral dilemma is resolvable by an ideal moral judge, there are certain dilemmas that are by no means readily resolved. However, beyond assigning differing weights to certain moral principles, ethical reflection provides some additional guidance that deals specifically with conflicts among principles and competing claims among individuals and groups.

Through centuries of reflection, a particular moral principle, justice, has given us such additional guidance. Justice as a moral principle is explicitly concerned with adjudicating conflict. In previous chapters we have already made reference to John Rawls's two principles of justice which serve to order competing claims. For our purposes, it will be enough here to illustrate only one type of situation in which competing claims arise and show why it is important to clarify our thinking both about what are the most weighty moral principles and also about our conception of justice, so that we have ways of dealing with situations in which immediate decisions must be made. The example I wish to use has to do with the allocation of medical resources.

Underlying ordinary medical practice is a notion of justice as fairness. Persons coming to doctors' offices or to hospitals generally receive appointments, are seen, or are admitted in the order in which the requests are made. The principle of first come, first served generally guides the allocation of medical services. Fairness is achieved by developing a queue and honoring its contractual arrangements. Within a given system of health care, however just otherwise, this avoids making services dependent upon the merit, social importance, dress, attractiveness, race, sex, productivity, religion, age, or whatever other characteristics may differentiate and characterize the various people seeking medical services. Of course, there are subtle institutional forms of discrimination, racial, sexual, or other, which are not necessarily overcome within the total system of health care delivery by this procedure.[6]

But on moral grounds, there is a well-understood exception to the rule that people will be served on a first come, first served basis and that the contracts made on this basis will be routinely honored. The admission of people for doctors' appointments or into hospitals will also depend upon whether or not any particular request being made involves an emergency. If in any instance a particular person requiring medical attention is in immediate danger of dying, that person will be given preference over others who are not in such immediate danger. Indeed, it is standard procedure in the emergency room to determine as quickly as possible the medical needs of patients and to treat first those who are most in need of care. How does one justify this apparent inequality of preferential treatment?

Presumably people would agree that saving a life is much more important than setting a broken arm or making sure that someone is physically fit who indeed appears to be. A right to life or the obligation to protect and save human life would seem to be much more important than any obligation to relieve momentary anxiety or pain. It would appear, then, that the liberty to save one's life is one that we will generally want to maximize, provided that what we do in this regard is compatible with a like liberty for others.

But justice demands that we treat those who are equally at risk as equally in need of medical services. Again, the principle of first come, first served among those who are equally at risk for death would be one way to achieve fairness under less than ideal circumstances where not everyone can be treated at the same time. However, if, strictly speaking, two people equally at risk of death need the one resource available to treat them at a particular point in time, it would seem that equalizing the risk of death could only be maintained by the toss of a coin or some such device for achieving an equal chance of treatment. Again, ideally such situations are not supposed to arise and for the most part, do not. In actual fact, though, a physician arriving at an accident scene may be confronted with two profusely bleeding victims and will, of course, only be able to diagnose and treat one at a time, and one of these will have to be the first one to be treated. Apparently physicians caught in these circumstances tend to follow a version of first come, first served as a principle by treating the first one they come upon and touch. Fairness would not be generally violated by this except that if one had some way of knowing at a glance or in advance that one of these victims was more at risk of death, obviously that one should be treated first. And if it were possible to determine quickly that both victims were equally at risk of death, a lottery would be the fairest.

But some people might press us further. Is a lottery always the best way to resolve dilemmas where a number of people are equally at risk of death? Or to put the question another way, should we always, without exception, equalize the right to life? Strictly speaking, this is precisely what we ought always to do if we are to observe Rawls's first principle of justice to provide for each person an equal right to the most extensive basic liberty compatible with like liberty for all, presuming that a right to life is one of those basic liberties that would be maximized. In chapter 5 we argued for the protection of life as one of the very basic and most stringent obligations of any society, and the injunction not to kill as the most stringent form of the principle of nonmaleficence.

Exceptions, then, to this general principle of equalizing the right to life would have to be such that this principle is not threatened by agreeing to a particular exception. A couple of examples should suffice for our purposes here—wartime provides one, a lifeboat situation the other.

In wartime, there may be certain circumstances in which soldiers who are most at risk of dying will not receive the preferential treatment that would most certainly be the morally right thing to do, other things being equal. It is quite conceivable that limited medical supplies could be used first on soldiers who have the best chance to return to combat. And only after such soldiers have been treated, would one see what is left for those who are least likely to respond to treatment. This cruel situation is brought about by one of the necessities of war, namely, to defend the lives of innocent people. From a moral standpoint, war would only be justified to ward off unjust aggression and to save the lives of those who would otherwise become victims of such unjust aggression.[7] Assuming now that a just war is being conducted, it may be the case at a given instance in such a war that too many lives would be risked by using scarce medical resources for the troops most at risk of dying rather than for troops who can soon be returned to combat for the sake of saving lives.[8] Under very carefully defined and specified circumstances, therefore, it may be argued that the usual way of satisfying an equal right to life so jeopardizes the lives of so many that the very preservation of life and numbers of lives becomes the overriding consideration.

It is very important not to see this example as hinging simply on the number of lives involved, although that is certainly an important consideration. The morally right act cannot be decided simply by deciding that two lives are better than one, and justifying inequality with respect to the right to life on that basis. For instance, suppose two armed policemen come upon a scene in which an innocent victim is about to be murdered by two armed assailants. If the only way to prevent the slaughter of an innocent person is to shoot the two armed assailants, then it certainly would be morally justified to risk killing both of these unjust aggressors to save the life of one innocent, would-be victim. Justice is indeed a complicated concept that includes at its core a notion of equal treatment and opportunity, but which involves as well considerations of need, and very strictly and carefully defined considerations of merit where merit is a morally relevant consideration. We have already noted this aspect of justice in chapter 5.

Turning now to lifeboat situations, consider one where it appears that the individuals in the lifeboat will starve before rescue is likely. One could argue that a mutually agreed upon lottery would be the only fair way to determine who among the passengers would be sacrificed so that the rest may have a chance to live. One might think of certain kinds of individuals whom passengers in the lifeboat might agree to exempt from the lottery on the grounds that the lives of everyone depend upon the survival of such individuals. For example, people in the lifeboat may feel strongly that a particular person who is the only one that knows how to guide the boat toward the nearest land should be exempted from a lottery. Nevertheless, it would be important that both the lottery and any such exemption from the lottery be mutually agreed upon. Otherwise the principle of maximizing individual liberty compatible with like liberty for all would be violated under circumstances where apparently one or the other cannot agree that their lives are best protected by either a lottery or by exempting a particular person from an otherwise agreed upon lottery. After all, in any lifeboat situation, each passenger has his or her own particular view regarding the necessity of any sacrifice of life, and if no regard is given to these differences in assessment, the enforcement of a sacrifice of one life or another can be seen as murder, however extenuating the circumstances.

We are not here, however, presuming that we have made a final case for a lottery in the kinds of situations depicted above. Courts have not always agreed on lotteries and readers who wish to pursue this further will find more extensive discussions elsewhere.[9] What we are rather trying to convey to readers by talking about justice under conditions where a lottery may be suitable is to illustrate how justice as a moral principle does serve to order severe conflicts and moral dilemmas, and how it does this in combination with considerations of what moral principles are generally most morally stringent. The value of justice in resolving conflict and establishing priorities is widely recognized and discussed in ethics, and goes quite beyond our particular discussion here.

There are surely major sources of past and continuing reflection upon what moral principles are most weighty, and what characterizes an ideal moral judge, which are not confined to ethics as a formal discipline. Religious traditions and institutions are among these. It is important, then, to consider the relationship between religion and morality and to say something about what religion may contribute to the moral life.

RELIGION AND MORALITY

Religious ethicists and religiously devout persons may feel that this book has not done justice to the special claims of religious traditions. In some respects, this is clearly so. Certainly we are vulnerable to the charge that we have not even attempted to indicate the many ways in which religious insights have in the past and do in the present influence in positive ways our ethical thought as well as the caliber of our moral behavior and character. Religious institutions have been, and continue to be, part of our social endeavor to improve both our knowledge of what is ethical and our will to do what is right and good. In no way has this book wished to deny this. Nor have we indulged in analyses of the history of failure in religious traditions. Sometimes religions have been influential in fostering war and prejudice as well as peace and impartial justice. What is important to note, however, is that religious and quasi-religious notions of reality do have a significant input into our particular moral judgments. This we illustrated somewhat in chapter 2.

Some readers may also ask about the special claims for religious insight or revelation. The view we have taken in this book is that all the great religious traditions have included in them the assumption that persons both within and without particular religious traditions are capable of recognizing right and wrong, good and evil, whatever influence may be imputed to religion and to religious communities.[10] Certainly religious communities can influence our very conceptions of what is right in very profound ways. Judaism and Christianity both rejected infanticide as practiced by Roman and Greek society. The wrongness of killing was definitely applied to the very earliest stages of life by traditions that saw the gift of life as something over which parents should not exercise tyrannical or absolute power. An ideal moral judge as conceived within Jewish and Christian traditions would place a positive value on even the most useless and seemingly insignificant forms of human life. Indeed, Nietzsche with his philosophy of the superman was utterly opposed to Judaism and Christianity on this very point.[11] The idea of treating relatively unproductive or incompetent people as equals was utterly abhorrent to Nietzsche, so that on these matters he found himself more at home in Greek and Roman attitudes.

But the claim to revelation raises issues far too complicated to be fully discussed here.[12] Let us note only that the general point of such claims is that in the moral sphere, there is knowledge that comes not only from specifically moral experience but from religious experience as well. Without in any way denying that religious experience and reflections on it may yield knowledge of our world, we have nevertheless restricted ourselves here to looking at certain aspects of moral discourse that lend themselves to open investigation by inquiring minds regardless of their particular religious experiences as individuals or as members of religious communities.

It is important to bear in mind also that religious claims require testing on moral as well as other scientific and intellectual grounds. I need not belabor the fact that it is possible to call certain religious beliefs and actions fanaticism from the standpoint of our more commonly held moral perceptions. The claim by the murderer of Martin Luther King, Jr.'s mother is one among many evil actions that persons have claimed were inspired by their views of God's will or some other specific religious conviction.

Nor need we remind the reader of Holy War and its terrors. Any claim, therefore, to have revelation should from a moral and intellectual point of view be subject to scrutiny. More reflective and systematic theologians have over the centuries recognized this and called for various kinds of rational and experiential verification of religious and moral claims made by religious writings and communities. Judaism and Christianity, for example, have applied stringent scientific intellectual methods to the study and understanding of their own scriptures so that whatever may be called revelation is clearly subject to systematic intellectual as well as experiential testing. One should not assume that talk about religious insight or revelation will issue in unverified or unverifiable dogma. Our neglect of all of these issues in this very short introduction is by no means a function of any negative view of religion and religious traditions. What we have done, however, does imply that we take a critical and nondogmatic view toward whatever claims to truth may come not only from religion but also from moral philosophy.

One of the enduring insights of religious traditions has been to cultivate certain intellectual abilities and personal characteristics that are essential to the moral life. Modern moral philosophy has tended to overlook this aspect of what it means to be morally conscientious and how it is that we could come to expect that people will recognize, as well as want to do, what is right and good. Ancient moral philosophers did share this concern with religious traditions. Recently this concern has re-expressed itself in moral philosophy. Although Frankena, in contrast to the view we are taking, does not consider these abilities as moral virtues, he does recognize as essential to the moral life "the ability to make moral decisions and to revise one's principles if necessary, and the ability to realize vividly, in imagination and feeling, the 'inner lives' of others." [13] What he goes on to say is something like a restatement of the Golden Rule: if we are to expect people to understand moral rules and principles, this will involve, among other things, "being a certain kind of person." And this in turn will entail that we attain and develop "an ability to be aware of others as persons, as important to themselves as we are to ourselves, and to have a lively and sympathetic representation in imagination of their interests and of the effects of our actions on their lives." [14] In effect, Frankena is saying that taking on some of the characteristics of an ideal observer is a morality-supporting thing to do. From the perspective developed in chapter 5, we have interpreted this as one of our moral obligations. It is an obligation that is very much recognized within religious traditions and there is a vast and rich literature on what it would mean to love and emulate God who is within such traditions an ideal moral judge having the qualities of which Frankena has been speaking.[15]

From one perspective, then, we could say that there is an obligation to try to realize in ourselves and others the kinds of ideal conditions expressed in our moral discourse and identified by Firth as characteristics of an ideal observer. From a religious perspective, we would want to think of such an ideal moral judge, not as a hypothetical being but as an actual being, namely, God. Such a being would be in part known to us but in part beyond our knowing, and worthy of our emulation and reverence on the basis not only of our moral experiences, but also other experiences of the nature of reality. Whether we take an explicitly religious or nonreligious view of these matters, it seems clear that morality will not be realized nor moral principles identified and followed if human individuals and groups have neither the desire nor the institutional means for developing the kind of sensitivities that an ideal moral judge would have.

CONCLUDING POSTSCRIPT

Recently I viewed and heard the Russian author and Nobel laureate Aleksandr Solzhenitsyn being interviewed. He expressed his deep concern that Western democracies appeared to be declining and may decline so much that they will be defeated, without a struggle, by Russia. Asked how the Western democracies may avert destruction from within and from without, Solzhenitsyn offered a simple yet profound reply: ''distinguish clearly between good and evil.'' This book has sought to stimulate its readers to do just that. With Solzhenitsyn, I believe that people generally have some will and some capacity to discern the differences between right and wrong, good and evil. Otherwise this book, like his admonition, would be futile or even absurd.

But if people generally have a willingness and a capacity for moral discernment, what urgency, apart from a desire to encourage and instruct, is there for an admonition such as

Solzhenitsyn's and for an introduction to ethics such as this one? In Solzhenitsyn's *The Gulag Archipelago,* the urgency for encouraging and instructing people to examine their moral reasoning is rather dramatically illustrated. In this book, Solzhenitsyn documents his major contention that certain forms of moral reasoning led to and accompanied the very actions allegedly justified by such reasoning. The passages that follow are taken from speeches in the Soviet court by Krylenko, the Prosecutor General after the Revolution. Solzhenitsyn explains that the revolutionary tribunal in many instances made no stenographic records, in other instances destroyed those that did exist. As a result, our only written evidence for what happened in the courts in the period under discussion (1918–1922) is contained in the prosecution speeches of Krylenko. These speeches state frankly and precisely the tasks of the Soviet courts when the court was "'at one and the same time both *the creator of the law* [Krylenko's italics] . . . *and a political weapon.'* (My italics.)''[16] Solzhenitsyn goes on to explain that Krylenko could view the court as the creator of the law because for four years there were no codes. The Tsarist codes had been thrown out. What follows now are some examples of Krylenko's own reasoning and Solzhenitsyn's analyses of them.

"A tribunal is not the kind of court in which fine points of jurisprudence and clever stratagems are to be restored. . . . We are creating a new law and *new ethical norms.*" And also: "No matter how much is said here about the eternal law of truth, justice, etc., we know . . . how dearly these have cost us."

(But if *your* prison terms are compared with *ours* maybe it didn't cost you so dearly after all? Maybe eternal justice was somewhat more comfortable?)

The reason that fine points of jurisprudence are unnecessary is that there is no need to clarify whether the defendant is guilty or not guilty: the concept of *guilt* is an old bourgeois concept which has now been uprooted.

And so we heard from Comrade Krylenko that a tribunal was *not that kind of court!* On another occasion we would hear from him that a tribunal was *not a court at all:* "A tribunal is an organ of the class struggle of the workers directed against their enemies" and must act "from the point of view of the interests of the revolution . . . having in mind *the most desirable results* for the masses of workers and peasants." People are not people, but "carriers of specific ideas." ". . . No matter what the individual qualities of the defendant, *only one* method of evaluating him is to be applied: evaluation from the point of view of *class expediency*."

In other words, you can exist only if it's expedient for the working class. And if "this expediency should require that the avenging sword should fall on the head of the defendants, then no . . . verbal arguments can help." (Such as arguments by lawyers, etc.) "In our revolutionary court we are guided not by articles of the law and not by the degree of extenuating circumstances; in the tribunal we must proceed on the basis of considerations of expediency."

That was the way it was in those years: people lived and breathed and then suddenly found out that their existence was *inexpedient*.

And it must also be kept in mind that it was not what he had done that constituted the defendant's burden, but what he *might* do if he were not shot now. "We protect ourselves not only against the past but also against the future."

Comrade Krylenko's pronouncements are clear and all-inclusive. They bring alive for us that whole period of the law in sharp relief. The clarity of autumn suddenly pierces the mists of spring and reaches us. And is it perhaps unnecessary to go further? Perhaps we aren't required to page through trial after trial. These pronouncements will be henceforth inexorably applied.[17]

Echoing Solzhenitsyn, is it necessary to go further? Should we multiply examples of the practical nature of moral reasoning? Solzhenitsyn did cite many examples of moral reasoning that were used to justify violating moral principles and he follows these with case after case of actually carrying out the violations previously justified in theory only. Surely all the readers have their own favorite examples of "justifications" used to violate moral principles. All of us in our daily lives are confronted by arguments based on expediency, and appeals to the greatest good for the greatest number, to the most desirable results, to a new ethic, and the like. The limitations of these simple and superficially plausible modes of reasoning need to be recognized and alternatives proposed and understood. A community that fails to do this will fail properly to distinguish good and evil in thought, and so also in practice.

Nor need I belabor long the practical significance of institutionalizing and defending criteria for achieving rational and impartial decisions. In chapter 7, we offered as one example of how ideal conditions for making moral judgments are at least partially institutionalized, a governmental system in which there is a separation of its judicial, legislative, and executive branches. It is no accident that in defending the whole process of suspending fair judicial procedures, civil rights, and summarily condemning many to death, Krylenko chose explicitly to reject the independence of the judiciary; he called such a separation of powers "a false theory."[18] Similarly, Sverdlov, chairman of the All-Russian Central Executive Committee, who could and did "correct" court sentences without leaving his office, alleged that "It is very good that the legislative and executive power are not divided by a thick wall as they are in the West."[19] Without speculating about the extent to which Krylenko and Sverdlov were knowingly justifying evil, or sincerely advocating a theory and practice that would best realize the greatest good as they saw it, or both, they chose to commend their actions publicly by attacking a method by which impartial justice has long been sought. And instead of suggesting alternative ways of achieving impartiality, they praised a policy that was purposely partial to one group and its interests at the expense of those deemed a threat to those interests. Their assaults on basic human rights and fair treatment were no deviation from the norm; these assaults were demanded by their theory of justifiable partiality for the ends they sought, however noble these actually seemed to them. Thus, what we can justify and what arguments we use are not idle, inconsequential matters. Even those who believe in the impartial administration of justice and the theories which make explicit how it is best realized will, particularly if they have power over others, find it difficult to think and act impartially. Actual systems of checks and balances of power are as indispensable as the right thinking that spawns and defends them if justice is to be a reality.

In the end, then, ethical reasoning is too important to be left to an elite group, whether this elite group be scholars, politicians, health professionals, lawyers, military experts, corporate executives, or any other kind of professional. The opportunity and the task of moral reasoning is for everyone. This book has been an introduction to that opportunity and that task.

notes

Chapter I

1. Ewing, *Ethics* (The English Universities Press Ltd., 1953), p. 1.
2. To assert that some characteristics of actions or policies, like keeping promises, are right-making is not to say that it would never be right in a specific instance to break a promise. Rather, it is to claim that an action would always be right insofar as it is an act of promise-keeping. In a given instance, an act of breaking a promise may be right because it is at the same time an act of saving a life, and saving a life is a right-making characteristic that has a greater moral claim upon us than the moral claim of keeping a promise. This point will receive further attention in chapter 6.
3. Potter, *War and Moral Discourse* (John Knox Press, 1969), p. 23.
4. *Ibid.*
5. *Ibid.*, pp. 26-28.
6. Lehmann, *Ethics in a Christian Context* (New York: Harper & Row, 1963).
7. William K. Frankena, *Ethics*, 2d. ed. (Englewood Cliffs, New Jersey: Prentice-Hall, Inc., 1973), p. 4.
8. See Reinhold Niebuhr, "General Essays on Love and Justice," in *Love and Justice*, ed. D. B. Robertson (Cleveland: The World Publishing Company, 1957), pp. 25-54.
9. "To a very large extent, it may be, Christianity represents a qualification of human practical existence, or at least of Western moral life, rather than a new and wholly different way of living; it may represent a species rather than a genus of human moral existence. If that is true, as many before us have believed, then the reflections of Christians on their life as agents will to no small extent coincide with, or otherwise be similar to, the reflections of some who are not Christians." (H. Richard Niebuhr, *The Responsible Self* [New York: Harper & Row, 1963], p. 150). Although we are using Christian ethics as an example of how religious ethics is a subspecies of ethics generally, there is no intent here to exclude the ethics of other world religions. Although there are important differences among world religions on matters of ethics, the working assumption of this book is that the quest for basic moral principles and rational moral discourse is common to the human community. The work of Lawrence Kohlberg, described most succinctly in "The Child as a Moral Philosopher," *Psychology Today* (September, 1968), pp. 25-30, suggests that there are important similarities in moral development across cultures. Work in comparative ethics is barely beginning and there is much to be done in this area. See, for example, the essays by David Little: "Calvin and the Prospects for a Christian Theory of Natural Law," in Outka and Ramsey, eds., *Norm and Context in Christian Ethics* (New York: Charles Scribner's Sons, 1968), pp. 175-97, and "Max Weber and the Comparative Study of Religious Ethics," *The Journal of Religious Ethics*, 2 (Fall, 1974), 5-40.
10. Franz J. Ingelfinger, "Bedside Ethics for the Hopeless Case," *New England Journal of Medicine* 289:17 (October 25, 1973), 914-15.
11. Edmund D. Pellegrino, "Reform and Innovation in Medical Education: The Role of Ethics," in Robert M. Veatch, Willard Gaylin, and Councilman Morgan, eds., *The Teaching of Medical Ethics* (New York: Institute of Society, Ethics and the Life Sciences, 1973), pp. 150-65.

Chapter II

1. The substance of what follows has also been published in *The Monist,* January 1977.
2. Ehrlich, *The Population Bomb* (Ballantine Books, Inc., 1968). See also Ehrlich and Anne Ehrlich, *Population, Resources, and Environment: Issues in Human Ecology* (W. H. Freeman, 1970).
3. W. Paddock and P. Paddock, *Famine 1975* (Little Brown & Co., 1967).
4. Garrett Hardin, "The Tragedy of the Commons," *Science,* 162, 1969, 1243-48.
5. Ehrlich, *The Population Bomb.*
6. Kingsley Davis, "Population Policy: Will Current Programs Succeed?" *Science,* 158 (1969), 730-39; Hardin, "The Tragedy of the Commons."
7. Edward Pohlman, "Incentives: Not Ideal, but Necessary," in J. Philip Wogaman, ed., *The Population Crisis and Moral Responsibility* (Public Affairs Press, 1973), pp. 225-32. For a non–crisis-oriented, careful sorting out of ethical issues raised by incentive policies, see Robert M. Veatch, "Governmental Incentives: Ethical Issues at Stake," *ibid.,* pp. 207-24.
8. Davis, "Population Policy: Will Current Programs Succeed?" and Ehrlich and Ehrlich, *Population, Resources, and Environment: Issues in Human Ecology.*
9. Paddock and Paddock, *Famine 1975.* See also Wade Greene, "Triage: Who Shall Be Fed? Who Shall Starve?" *New York Times Magazine* (January 9, 1975); this essay cites the Paddocks, Hardin, and Ehrlich, among others.
10. Melvin M. Ketchel, "Fertility Control Agents as a Possible Solution to the World Population Problem," *Perspect. Biol. Med.* 11 (1968), 687-703.
11. See Ralph B. Potter, "The Simple Structure of the Population Debate: The Logic of the Ecology Movement," in Robert M. Veatch, ed., *Population Policy and Ethics: The American Tradition* (New York: Irvington Press: 1977), for a fuller discussion of these issues.
12. Phyllis Tilson Piotrow, *World Population Crisis: The United States Response* (Praeger Publishers, 1973). Annually since 1969, the Population Council has published reviews of family-planning activities in governments around the world. See, for example, Dorothy Nortman and Ellen Hofstatter, "Population and Family Planning Programs: A Factbook," *Reports on Population/Family Planning,* December, 1974.
13. Piotrow, *World Population Crisis: The United States Response.*
14. *Population and the American Future: The Report of the Commission on Population Growth and the American Future* (New York: Signet Book, New American Library, Inc., 1972); Philander P. Claxton, Jr., and Marjorie A. Costa, *Statement by the Delegation of the United States of America,* Second Asian Population Conference, Tokyo, November 1-13, 1972; *U. S. Aid to Population/Family Planning in Asia,* Report of a Staff Survey Team to the Committee on Foreign Affairs, U.S. House of Representatives, 93rd Congress, 1st Session, February 25, 1973 (Washington, D.C.: U.S. Government Printing Office, 1973); *United States of America Country Statement,* in response to the United Nations Second Inquiry Among Governments on Population Growth and Development (submitted by the Department of State, June, 1973); "United Nations World Population Year and Conference, 1974," draft of pamphlet prepared by U.S. State Department, 1973.
15. There are numerous articles in the various publications of the Population Council, particularly discussions of KAP (Knowledge, Attitudes and

Practices) studies that seek to document these contentions. See, also, *Population and the American Future*. For a criticism of KAP studies and the conclusions drawn from them, see Anthony Marino, "KAP Surveys and the Politics of Family Planning," *Concerned Demography*, 3 (Fall, 1971), 36-75.

16. *Population and the American Future*, pp. 1-2.

17. *Ibid.*, p. 188.

18. *Ibid.*, pp. 72-73.

19. *Ibid.*, chap. 11.

20. The Bucharest World Plan of Action has been reprinted in an appendix to "A Report on Bucharest," *Studies in Family Planning*, 5 (December, 1974) (New York: The Population Council).

21. Roger Revelle, "Paul Ehrlich: New High Priest of Ecocatastrophe," *Family Planning Perspectives*, 3 (April, 1971), 68. Revelle has calculated how many people would have been needed in the United States in 1965 to keep pollution levels precisely where they were in 1940: "Other things being equal, the number of automobiles and the amount of gasoline and paper consumed would have remained about constant over the quarter century if our population had declined from 133 million people in 1940 to 67 million in 1965. To maintain a constant flow of sulphur dioxide in the air from electric power plants, the population would have had to decrease to only 40 million people. Presumably the amount of nitrogen fertilizers would not have increased, if all but 17 million Americans had reemigrated to the homes of their ancestors. Only 17 million people in the country would use the same amount of nitrogen in 1965 as we used in 1940. The national parks would have remained as uncrowded in 1965 as they were in 1940 if our population during the interval had gone down from 130 million people in 1940 to 30 million people in 1965, instead of going up to 195 million as, of course, it actually did." Roger Revelle (testimony), *Effects of Population Growth on Natural Resources and the Environment*, Hearings before the Reuss Subcommittee on Conservation and Natural Resources (Washington, D.C.: U. S. Government Printing Office, 1969).

22. B. M. Bhatia, *Famines in India: 1860–1965* (New York: Asia Publishing House, 1967); James Gavan and John Dixon, "The Food Situation in India: A Perspective," (essay, Harvard Center for Population Studies, October, 1974). See also Roger Revelle, "Food and Population," in *Scientific American*, 231 (September, 1974).

23. John B. Wyon and John E. Gordon, *The Khanna Study* (Cambridge: Harvard University Press, 1971).

24. Revelle, "Food and Population."

25. Revelle, "Paul Ehrlich: New High Priest of Ecocatastrophe."

26. Appendix to "A Report on Bucharest," *Studies in Family Planning*.

27. William Rich, *Smaller Families Through Social and Economic Progress*, Monograph No. 7 of the Overseas Development Council, Washington, D. C., January, 1973, p. 37. See also James Kocher, *Rural Development, Income Distribution and Fertility Decline*, an occasional paper of the Population Council (Bridgeport, Conn.: Key Book Service, 1973).

28. Dudley Kirk, "A New Demographic Transition?" in *Rapid Population Growth: Consequences and Policy Implications* (Baltimore: Johns Hopkins Press, 1971), pp. 123-47.

29. Population Council literature contains many such articles. See also R. T. Ravenholt, James W. Brackett, and John Chao, "Family Planning Programs and Fertility Patterns," *Family Planning Programs*, Population Report,

Series J, No. 1 (August, 1973) (Department of Medical and Public Affairs, The George Washington University Medical Center).

30. Michael S. Teitelbaum, "Population and Development: Is a Consensus Possible?" *Foreign Affairs,* July, 1974, pp. 742-60.

31. Rich, *Smaller Families Through Social and Economic Progress;* Kocher, *Rural Development, Income Distribution and Fertility Decline;* William W. Murdoch and Allen Oaten, "Population and Food: Metaphors and the Reality," *BioScience* 25 (1975), 561-67.

32. Wyon and Gordon, *The Khanna Study.*

33. John C. Cobb, Harry M. Roulet, and Paul Harper, "An I.U.D. Field Trial in Lulliani, West Pakistan," paper presented at the American Public Health Association, October 21, 1965.

34. Wyon and Gordon, *The Khanna Study.* See also Robert Repetto, "The Interaction of Fertility and the Size Distribution of Income," research paper no. 8, Harvard Center for Population Studies (October 1974), and Rich, *Smaller Families Through Social and Economic Progress.*

35. See, e.g., the discussion of Marx and Marxism in Warren S. Thompson and David T. Lewis, *Population Problems* (New York: McGraw-Hill, 1965), pp. 48-51; official Roman Catholic affinity for stressing the centrality of social justice as a population policy can best be gleaned from Pope Paul VI's Encyclical, *Populorum Progressio* (Boston: Daughters of St. Paul, 1967).

36. Ehrlich and Ehrlich, *Population, Resources, and Environment: Issues in Human Ecology;* Revelle, "Paul Ehrlich: New High Priest of Ecocatrastrophe."

37. J. Bronowski, *Science and Human Values,* rev. ed. (New York: Harper & Row, 1965), pp. 65, 66.

38. Hardin, "The Tragedy of the Commons;" see also his "Living on a Lifeboat," *BioScience* 24 (1974), 561-68.

39. Murdoch and Oaten, "Population and Food: Metaphors and the Reality."

40. Robert Coles, *Children of Crisis* (Boston: Atlantic-Little-Brown, 1964), p. 369.

41. John Rawls, *A Theory of Justice* (The Belknap Press of Harvard University Press, 1971), p. 60.

Chapter III

1. J. A. T. Robinson, *Christian Morals Today* (London: SCM, 1964), pp. 18, 16.

2. *The Philosophy of John Stuart Mill,* ed. Marshall Cohen (New York: Random House, 1961), "Utilitarianism."

3. Jeremy Bentham, *Introduction to the Principles of Morals and Legislation,* 1789.

4. *The Philosophy of John Stuart Mill,* Cohen, "Utilitarianism," p. 342.

5. *Ibid.,* chap. 5.

6. Joseph Fletcher, *Situation Ethics* (Philadelphia: Westminster Press, 1966), p. 95.

7. *Ibid.,* pp. 57-68; pp. 98-99.

8. W. D. Ross, *The Right and the Good* (Oxford: Clarendon, 1930).

9. *Ibid.,* p. 17.

10. *Ibid.*

11. *Ibid.,* p. 18.

12. *Ibid.,* pp. 19-20.

13. *Ibid.,* p. 21. I am not accepting Ross's formulation of moral principles in every respect. Certain inadequacies in Ross's formulations of justice, beneficence, and nonmaleficence will be discussed in chapters 4 and 5.

14. Paul Taylor, *Principles of Ethics: An Introduction* (Encino, California: Dickinson Publishing Company, 1975), pp. 63-64; for Taylor, moral rules other than that of seeking the maximum happiness (pleasure) have no intrinsic value. It is difficult to see the practical difference, then, between act and rule utilitarianism, as we argue later in this chapter. In *Ethics*, pp. 37-43, Frankena not only distinguishes act utilitarianism and rule utilitarianism but also general utilitarianism. He notes also that there are those who have contended that all three of these views are logically or ultimately equivalent to act utilitarianism. For a rather convincing case, see David Lyons, *Forms and Limits of Utilitarianism* (London: Oxford University Press, 1965). It would take us too far afield to discuss all of these intricate, philosophical issues. The arguments I am offering against rule utilitarianism do, I think, count against all forms of utilitarianism. However, those readers who wish to explore utilitarianism further should see Dan Brock, "Recent Work in Utilitarianism," *American Philosophical Quarterly*, 10 (October, 1973), pp. 241-76, and also Richard B. Brandt, "Toward a Credible Form of Utilitarianism," in *Morality and the Language of Conduct*, ed. Hector-Neri Castañeda and George Nakhnikian (Detroit: Wayne State University Press, 1963), pp. 107-44.
15. Taylor, *Principles of Ethics: An Introduction*, p. 64.
16. *Ibid.*, p. 79.
17. *Ibid.*, p. 66.
18. *Ibid.*, p. 63.
19. Lyons, *Forms and Limits of Utilitarianism*. See also Dan Brock for other references on this issue.

Chapter IV

1. W. D. Ross, *The Right and the Good* (Oxford: Clarendon, 1930), p. 21.
2. William K. Frankena, *Ethics*, 2d ed. (Englewood Cliffs, N.J.: Prentice-Hall, Inc., 1973), p. 47.
3. For a discussion of the just-war criteria, see Ralph B. Potter, Jr., "The Moral Logic of War," paper delivered at Occidental College, Los Angeles, California, November, 1969, and published as "Occasional Paper No. 5 on the Church and Conflict" by the Department of Church and Society, Board of Christian Education, United Presbyterian Church U.S.A. See also Paul Ramsey, *The Just War* (New York: Charles Scribner's Sons, 1968).
4. *Webster's New World Dictionary* (Second College Edition), ed. David B. Guralnik (Englewood Cliffs, N.J.: Prentice-Hall, Inc., The World Publishing Company, 1970), p. 484.
5. See Marvin Kohl, "Understanding the Case for Beneficent Euthanasia," in *Science, Medicine and Man*, Vol. 1, 1973, pp. 111-21, and "Beneficent Euthanasia" in *The Humanist* (July/August, 1974), pp. 9-11.
6. Kohl, "Understanding the Case for Beneficent Euthanasia," pp. 112–13.
7. *Ibid.*, p. 113.
8. B. D. Colen, "Doctors Decide on Life Support End," *Washington Post*, March 10, 1974.
9. It should be noted that the official Roman Catholic Hospital Regulations in this country, though explicitly opposed to euthanasia, are concerned to specify that physicians and hospital staff are definitely permitted to give pain relief, even when it is recognized that this will shorten the life of an imminently dying patient. Of course, as in all medical interventions, the consent of the patient is necessary.

10. In chapter 6 we will be discussing the difference between saying that something is a wrong-making characteristic of actions as compared with saying that something is always wrong. Actions are complex and may be wrong in certain respects and right in others, and in our actual moral decisions we often have to decide of any action whether it is the most right or the least wrong thing to do in a given situation.

11. Strictly speaking, the Mosaic covenant prohibits "murder" rather than killing as such. This indicates that from the point of view of this agreement not to kill, killing may sometimes be morally justified, when, for example, it is a matter of self-defense or intervention on behalf of an innocent life against an aggressor. The Mosaic covenant will be discussed in more detail in chapter 5.

12. See note 9.

13. Dr. Elisabeth Kübler-Ross, who is an opponent of beneficent euthanasia but a staunch proponent and practitioner of kindness in the form of relief of suffering, has provided one important model of care for dying persons. See her book *Death and Dying* (New York: Macmillan, 1969). There are also organizations like Hospice, first organized in England and now functioning in the United States as well. Information about Hospice may be obtained from Hospice, Incorporated, New Haven, Connecticut.

14. See chapter 3 of Paul Ramsey, *The Patient as Person* (New Haven: Yale University Press, 1970), pp. 113-64.

15. See the discussion of the principle of beneficence in Frankena, *Ethics,* pp. 45-48.

Chapter V

1. The story of the Good Samaritan obviously includes as well the whole idea of loving God. The importance of that notion both from a secular and a religious perspective will be part of the discussion in chapter 8. For a rather thorough contemporary description of a variety of ways in which love of neighbor has been understood in Christian ethics, see Gene Outka, *Agape* (New Haven: Yale University Press, 1972).

2. Biblical scholars since the work of G. E. Mendenhall contend that the language and form in which the Mosaic covenant occurs are those of a typical suzerainty treaty between a people and their ruler. See G. E. Mendenhall, *Law and Covenant in Israel and the Ancient Near East* (Pittsburgh: The Biblical Colloquium, 1955).

3. For the importance of the family and socialization, see Talcott Parsons, *Social Structure and Personality* (New York: Macmillan, 1964), chap. 3, "The Incest Taboo in Relation to Social Structure and the Socialization of the Child," pp. 57-77. See also John Rawls, *A Theory of Justice* (Cambridge, Mass.: Belknap Press of Harvard University Press, 1971), pp. 453-512.

4. Talcott Parsons, Renée C. Fox, and Victor M. Lidz, "The 'Gift of Life' and Its Reciprocation," *Social Research* 39 (1972), pp. 367-415. See also Arthur J. Dyck, "Procreative Rights and Population Policy," *Hastings Center Studies,* 1 (1973), pp. 74-82. The basic moral understanding of gift-giving and its reciprocation is pervasive and found also in very archaic societies. See Marcel Mauss, *The Gift* (New York: W. W. Norton & Company, Inc., 1967).

5. H. L. A. Hart, *The Concept of Law* (London: Oxford University Press, 1961), Chapter IX, "Laws and Morals," pp. 181-207.

6. Calvin has a rather dynamic conception of natural law based on the Mosaic covenant. See David Little, "Calvin and the Prospects for a Christian Theory

of Natural Law,'' in Outka and Ramsey, eds., *Norm and Context in Christian Ethics* (New York: Charles Scribner's Sons, 1968), pp. 175-97.

7. Sigmund Freud, *Civilization and Its Discontents,* trans. and ed. James Strachey (New York: W. W. Norton, 1961).

8. See note 3, where the importance of fidelity in marriage is related to the socialization and moral development of children.

9. There are numerous examples in Hosea and Amos.

10. A recent notable exception is Rawls, *A Theory of Justice*, which is much more akin to ancient philosophy with its concern for institutions and institutional relations.

11. Note how specifically the ideal community and its institutions are delineated in Plato's *Republic* and Bacon's *Atlantis,* to cite only two examples of utopian thinking.

12. W. D. Ross, *The Right and the Good* (Oxford: Clarendon, 1930), p. 21.

13. A recent work by Bernard Gert, *The Moral Rules* (New York: Harper & Row, Harper Torchbook Edition, 1973) is a distinct exception in the philosophical literature.

14. See the section entitled ''A Problem of Application'' in William K. Frankena, *Ethics* (Englewood Cliffs, New Jersey: Prentice-Hall, Inc., second edition, 1973), pp. 53-54.

15. J. A. T. Robinson, *Christian Morals Today* (London: SCM, 1964), p. 16.

16. Rawls, *A Theory of Justice,* chapter 8, ''The Sense of Justice,'' pp. 453-512.

17. See, for example, David A. Goslin, ed., *Handbook of Socialization Theory and Research* (Rand McNally & Co., 1969). Note the essay by Lawrence Kohlberg (''Stage and Sequence: The Cognitive-Developmental Approach to Socialization'') in which he is rather critical of the usual assumptions about the significance of parental figures for moral development. In contrast to Kohlberg, Erik Erikson has given a prominent role to parental figures in moral development: *Childhood and Society,* rev. ed. (New York: W. W. Norton Co., 1964).

18. See, for example, Ray E. Helfer and C. Henry Kempe, eds., *The Battered Child,* 2d ed. (Chicago: University of Chicago Press, 1974), and David G. Gil, *Violence Against Children* (Cambridge: Harvard University Press, 1970).

19. Raymond S. Duff and A. G. M. Campbell, ''Moral and Ethical Dilemmas in the Special-Care Nursery,'' *The New England Journal of Medicine,* 289 (October 25, 1973), 890-94.

20. Thomas Hobbes, *Leviathan,* 1651.

21. Michael LaChat, ''Utilitarian Reasoning in Nazi Medical Policy: Some Preliminary Investigations,'' *Linacre Quarterly,* 42 (February, 1975), 14-37.

22. See Preston N. Williams, ''James Cone and the Problem of a Black Ethic,'' in *Harvard Theological Review,* 65:4 (October, 1972), 483-94, for a discussion of fidelity in promising to protect and acknowledge the rights of blacks in the U.S. Constitution as requisite to trust and cooperation between blacks and whites.

23. Rawls, *A Theory of Justice.*

24. Frankena, *Ethics,* pp. 48-52.

25. Rawls, *A Theory of Justice,* p. 83; for a contemporary utilitarian alternative to Rawls, see Richard B. Brandt, *Ethical Theory* (Englewood Cliffs, N.J.: Prentice-Hall, Inc., 1959), chapter 16, ''Distributive Justice,'' pp. 407-32.

26. Ross, *The Right and the Good,* p. 21.

27. Bernard Bard and Joseph Fletcher, "The Right to Die," *The Atlantic Monthly* (April, 1968), p. 64.
28. Joseph Fletcher, "Indicators of Humanhood," *The Hastings Center Report* (November, 1972), 1-4.
29. Ross, *The Right and the Good,* pp. 24-26.
30. Gert, *The Moral Rules,* p. 72.
31. Frankena, *Ethics,* p. 62.
32. Frankena, *Ethics,* chap. 5.
33. Gert, *The Moral Rules,* p. 73.
34. Frankena, *Ethics,* chap. 4.
35. Arthur J. Dyck, "A Unified Theory of Virtue and Obligation," *The Journal of Religious Ethics,* I (Fall, 1973), pp. 37-52.

Chapter VI

1. J. A. T. Robinson, *Christian Morals Today* (London: SCM, 1964), p. 16.
2. Charles L. Stevenson, *Facts and Values* (New Haven: Yale University Press, 1963), p. 77.
3. Dietrich Bonhoeffer, *Ethics,* Eberhard Bethge, ed. (London: SCM, 1955); Paul Lehmann, *Ethics in a Christian Context* (New York: Harper & Row, 1963).
4. W. D. Ross, *The Right and the Good* (Oxford: Clarendon, 1930), pp. 19-20.
5. As we noted in chapter 5, the stringency of a particular duty may not only be due to the particular circumstances in which it occurs, but also for reasons discussed there, some duties (moral principles) are more stringent as such.
6. A. Biéler, *The Social Humanism of Calvin* (1961) (Richmond, Virginia: John Knox Press, 1964), pp. 54-58. Calvin always opposed interest on a loan made to the poor: ". . . it is illicit to receive interest from a poor man even when the law permits it" (*Ibid.,* p. 57).
7. Joseph Sittler, *The Structure of Christian Ethics* (Baton Rouge: Louisiana State University Press, 1958).
8. The reader should not conclude that saving the most lives is always the right thing to do. If, for example, two murderous robbers were about to shoot a single victim, it would be morally justifiable for two policemen who came upon this scene to shoot the two would-be murderers in order to save one innocent life. Other things being equal, we do justify killing aggressors who threaten people's lives, and in such a case, we would not hesitate to stop two aggressors for the sake of one innocent life.
9. As we noted in chapter 1, "A moral tragedy occurs when, after you have acted in a certain way and reflected on how you have acted, you come to the conclusion that, upon reflection, had you thought about it before you acted, you would have acted differently."
10. In chapter 3 we defined moral principles as constitutive rules, constitutive rules being rules that are "requisite to the very processes of formulating or deciding upon rules." See pp. 52-54 of chapter 3 for a fuller discussion of constitutive rules.
11. Max Wertheimer, "Some Problems in the Theory of Ethics" (1935), in M. Henle, ed., *Documents of Gestalt Psychology* (Berkeley: University of California, 1961); Karl Duncker, "Ethical Relativity," *Mind 48* (1939), 39-57.
12. S. E. Asch, *Social Psychology* (Englewood Cliffs, N.J.: Prentice-Hall, 1952), p. 377.

13. Duncker, "Ethical Relativity."
14. *Ibid.*, p. 50.
15. Richard Brandt, *Ethical Theory* (Englewood Cliffs, N.J.: Prentice-Hall, 1959), pp. 101-03.
16. *Ibid.*, p. 103.
17. "The anthropological evidence, taken by itself, then, does not give a *conclusive* answer to our question. At the present time, the anthropologist does not have two social groups of which he can say definitely: 'These groups have exactly the same beliefs about action A, on all points that could be seriously viewed as ethically relevant. . . . '" *Ibid.*, p. 284.
18. William Graham Sumner, *Folkways* (Boston: Ginn and Company, 1906); Ruth Benedict, "Anthropology and the Abnormal," *Journal of General Psychology 10* (1934), 59-80.
19. Edward Westermarck, *Ethical Relativity* (1932) (Paterson, N.J.: Littlefield, Adams & Co., 1960).
20. Bernard Williams, *Morality: An Introduction to Ethics* (New York: Harper & Row, 1972), pp. 1-12.
21. Brandt, *Ethical Theory,* pp. 275-78.
22. In *Ethical Theory,* p. 277, Brandt argues that emotivists have generally been methodological relativists. However, as he also indicates, emotive theory need not accept methodological relativism. Stevenson *(Facts and Values,* pp. 84-93) denies that his emotivist theory accepts or need accept methodological relativism.
23. Cited in Brandt, *Ethical Theory,* p. 288.

Chapter VII

1. G. P. Adams, "The Basis of Objective Judgments in Ethics," *International Journal of Ethics,* 37 (1927), 134-35.
2. Bertrand Russell, *Human Society in Ethics and Politics* (New York: New American Library, 1962), p. 19.
3. G. E. Moore, *Principia Ethica* (Cambridge: University Press, 1903).
4. Ross, *The Right and the Good* (Oxford: Clarendon, 1930), pp. 29-33.
5. Charles L. Stevenson, *Ethics and Language* (New Haven: Yale University Press, 1944).
6. Charles L. Stevenson, "The Emotive Meaning of Ethical Terms" (1937), in W. Sellars and J. Hospers, eds., *Readings in Ethical Theory* (New York: Appleton-Century-Crofts, 1952), p. 418.
7. Stevenson, *Ethics and Language,* chap. 2.
8. William K. Frankena, *Ethics,* 2d. ed. (Englewood Cliffs, N.J.: Prentice-Hall, 1973), p. 108.
9. *Ibid.*, pp. 113-14.
10. The term *naturalism* is a peculiar use of language restricted here to a particular metaethical view. In subscribing to naturalism in metaethics, one is in no way deciding metaphysical and/or religious questions. Naturalism, for example, need not be opposed either to theism or to the existence of what some may call "supernatural" phenomena.
11. Roderick Firth, "Ethical Absolutism and the Ideal Observer," *Philosophy and Phenomenological Research,* 12 (March, 1952), 326.
12. *Ibid.*
13. *Ibid.*, pp. 317-45.
14. In Firth's description of disinterestedness and dispassionateness, he makes a distinction between general interests and general passions on the one hand and

particular interests and particular passions on the other. The ideal observer has general interests and passions because particular interests and passions have a distorting effect upon our moral judgments. For example, if person Y is jealous of person X, then Y's judgments of X's character are likely to be incorrect unless such judgments are made in such a way that the feelings of jealousy have no influence in the making of such judgments. Judgments that discount a particular passion like jealousy, then, may be said to be dispassionate. In practice, however, it is very difficult to distinguish a particular passion from a general passion. Is love for one's spouse a particular passion, and love for people of the opposite sex a general passion? To be completely devoid of love either for one's spouse or for people of the opposite gender would in both instances distort moral judgments and presumably in the wrong direction. On the other hand, to be devoid of hatred in both of these instances may be a necessity for achieving correct moral judgments in actions affecting spouses and persons of the opposite gender. Considering the difficulties that we could easily multiply, it seems best to take the view that an ideal moral judge would be disinterested and dispassionate in the sense that the interests and passions of all parties affected by an action are taken into account, and at the same time, such an ideal moral judge has all the passions and interests necessary to do so and has all the knowledge and vivid imagination to discount interests and passions that in particular cases would block the possibility of discerning and feeling how all parties affected by a given action are in fact affected. Certain problems of Firth's delineation of disinterestedness and dispassionateness have also been discussed in Charles H. Reynolds, "Elements of a Decision Procedure for Christian Social Ethics," *Harvard Theological Review*, 65 (October, 1972), 509-30.

15. For a description of this NIH policy, see William J. Curran, "Governmental Regulation of the Use of Human Subjects in Medical Research: The Approach of Two Federal Agencies," in Paul A. Freund, ed., *Experimentation with Human Subjects* (New York: George Braziller, 1969), pp. 402-54.

16. Ralph B. Potter, *War and Moral Discourse* (Richmond: John Knox Press, 1969), chap. 2.

17. John Rawls, *A Theory of Justice* (Cambridge, Mass.: The Belknap Press of Harvard University Press, 1971).

18. It is not correct to link the ideal observer theory with utilitarianism, as Rawls did in his book *A Theory of Justice* (see pp. 183-92). Although it is correct that an ideal observer would, like a utilitarian, weigh the interests of various parties affected by an action, this would only be part of what an ideal observer would be doing in order to arrive at the most rational perception of what is fitting or right. Considerations of interests are not, by themselves and apart from the other ideal conditions specified by the ideal observer theory, determinative or right-making. The nature of the psychological, perceptual experience of an ideal observer is described in Arthur J. Dyck, "A Gestalt Analysis of the Moral Data and Certain of Its Implications for Ethical Theory," Ph.D. thesis, Harvard University (November, 1965). (This thesis will appear in a more refined and elaborated form in a forthcoming work, *Experiential Roots of the Moral Life.)*

Chapter VIII

1. J. Bronowski, *Science and Human Values* (New York: Harper & Row, 1972).
2. *Ibid.*, p. 65.
3. *Ibid.*, p. 66.

4. *Ibid.*
5. We refer here again to the characteristics of an ideal observer as described in Roderick Firth, "Ethical Absolutism and the Ideal Observer," *Philosophy and Phenomenological Research,* 12 (March, 1952), 317-45.
6. One important document on the more hidden forms of injustice within a total system of health care delivery is Charles V. Willie, Bernard M. Kramer, and Bertram S. Brown, eds., *Racism and Mental Health* (University of Pittsburgh Press, 1973). Gene Outka, "Social Justice and Equal Access to Health Care," *The Journal of Religious Ethics,* 2 (Spring, 1974), 11-32, provides an excellent analysis of how concepts of justice apply to systems of health care.
7. For a discussion of the just war criteria, see Ralph B. Potter, "The Moral Logic of War," paper delivered at Occidental College, Los Angeles, California, November, 1969, and published as "Occasional Paper No. 5 on the Church and Conflict" by the Department of Church and Society, Board of Christian Education, United Presbyterian Church U.S.A. See also Paul Ramsey, *The Just War* (New York: Charles Scribner's Sons, 1968).
8. An actual instance of this kind of situation is briefly discussed by Paul Freund in his introduction to the book he edited, *Experimentation with Human Subjects* (New York: George Braziller, 1969), p. xvii. Freund interprets the failure to treat soldiers wounded in battle and the preference given to soldiers with venereal disease as based on social utility. Depending on the total circumstances, this action may have also been justified on formalist grounds, although with more difficulty; and, we would contend, it should be very difficult to justify. Interestingly enough, Freund follows this case with an examination of renal dialysis and argues for the cogency of using lotteries or priority in time under certain circumstances.
9. See Paul Ramsey, *The Patient as Person* (New Haven: Yale University Press, 1970), chap. 7, for an analysis of how to choose among patients where medical supplies are limited, and the role of lotteries in such choices. He notes that U.S. maritime law prescribes casting lots among passengers apparently bound to die in an overloaded lifeboat. In *United States v. Holmes,* this use of a lottery was sanctioned as the procedure by means of which the equal respect for an equal right to life can be manifested when not all can be saved (p. 253). However, English law has tended to reject a human lottery in favor of waiting to die or be rescued (p. 253). English law, like American law, has not in such instances approved of making judgments of comparative social worthiness to reach decisions as to who will live or die. See also James Childress, "Who Shall Live When Not All Can Live," *Soundings,* 53 (Winter, 1970), 339-62.
10. For this view, see Larry K. Nelson, "The Independence of Moral from Religious Discourse in the Believer's Use of Language, *Harvard Theological Review,* 68 (April, 1975), 167-95; James M. Gustafson, *Can Ethics Be Christian?* (Chicago: University of Chicago Press, 1975); and David Sidorsky, "The Autonomy of Moral Objectivity," in Marvin Fox, ed., *Modern Jewish Ethics* (Ohio State University Press, 1975), pp. 153-73. For a broad range of thinking on the relation of religion and morality among moral philosophers and religious ethicists, see Gene Outka and John P. Reeder, Jr., *Religion and Morality* (Garden City, N.Y.: Doubleday Anchor Press, 1973).
11. Friedrich Nietzsche, *The Geneology of Morals* (1887), Francis Golffing, trans., (Garden City, N.Y.: Doubleday & Co., 1956), pp. 147-299.
12. A classic on revelation is H. R. Niebuhr, *The Meaning of Revelation* (New York: The MacMillan Company, 1941). See also James M. Gustafson, "The

Place of Scripture in Christian Ethics: A Methodological Study," *Interpretation,* 24 (1970), pp. 430-55.

13. William K. Frankena, *Ethics,* 2d. ed. (Englewood Cliffs, N.J.: Prentice-Hall, 1973), p. 69.

14. *Ibid.*

15. For a more detailed analysis of love of God as an obligation, see Arthur J. Dyck, "A Unified Theory of Virtue and Obligation," *The Journal of Religious Ethics,* 1 (Fall, 1973), 37-52, and "Referent-Models of Loving: A Philosophical and Theological Analysis of Love in Ethical Theory and Moral Practice," *Harvard Theological Review,* 61 (October, 1968), 525-45. This latter article shows how love of God as emulation of an ideal moral judge is enjoined in the Mosaic covenant. It should be noted that I have not interpreted as a normative principle the injunction in the Mosaic covenant not to covet, "envy," (Ex. 20:17; Deut. 5:21.) Envy distorts our efforts at impartiality and, hence, makes us something less than an ideal moral judge. John Rawls, *A Theory of Justice* (Cambridge, Mass.: The Belknap Press of Harvard University Press, 1971), has explicitly discussed the distorting effect of envy on judgments of what is just or unjust.

16. Aleksandr I. Solzhenitsyn, *The Gulag Archipelago* (New York: Harper & Row, 1973), pp. 307-8.

17. *Ibid.,* pp. 308-9.

18. *Ibid.,* p. 307.

19. *Ibid.*

Index